Born Deaf to an MBE

Shezad Nawab

Copyright © 2022

All Rights Reserved

ISBN: 9798401341891

Dedication

This book is dedicated to entrepreneurs from the deaf and hearing communities to instill confidence within their hearts.

Testimonials

"Shezad is a very creative and innovative entrepreneur."

- Sir Eric Peacock, Serial Entrepreneur.

"Shezad is a wonderful person with rich experience in entrepreneurship who overcomes challenges and is a role model to many."

-Shalini Khemka, Founder of E2Exchange.

"If I remember correctly, I have known Shezad for about six years, to date 2021. He first approached me with some queries and struggles for the Hard of Hearing community and told me that he wanted to support them by providing his services. So, I guided him to write to his M.P. at the time Caroline Spelman, now Dame. She supported his queries and introduced him to the then Chancellor, The Rt Hon Sajid Javid M.P. Within the same year, Shezad was fortunate to be honored by The Queen with an MBE. He has and will continue to excel. I commend him to greater heights on the publishing of his book."

- H.E. Yuvraj Ravendrasinh Thakor FOIE, CEO of Anantam Wealth.

"Shezad is an inspirational, hard-working, and incredibly talented individual. I have rarely come across someone more dedicated to equality of opportunity and someone widely regarded as a positive role model for many others."

-Cllr. Waseem Zaffar MBE, Cabinet Member, Transport and Environment.

"I had the pleasure of meeting Shezad in 2015 at a Disabled Entrepreneurs event held by Kaleidoscope Investments. When he first got up to present, his charisma and gravitas were profound. He communicated with confidence and empowered the audience that was listening to him. During our business dealings, I have had the privilege to observe his tenacity and hunger for success. His persistence is second to none, and his resilience is powerful. He is always thinking from a distinct angle and reaching out to people to connect. He has been positive and forward-looking during all the years that I have known him, and it's been an absolute pleasure to work with him."

-Hardeep Rai, Group Chief Executive Officer at The Kaleidoscope Group of Companies.

"Shezad enjoys a balanced and strong mindset and always overcame obstacles with ease. With such a strong mind, situations become opportunities, which is the foundation of his success."

-Paul Radway, Advertising, Senior Lecturer of Business School, Birmingham City University.

"Shezad has accumulated several significant entrepreneurial experiences over the years. As a deaf businessman who broke through the typical stereotypes, he is a true inspiration, an excellent role model, showing others that if he can achieve so much despite such difficulties, then they can do it too. I congratulate Shezad on coming this far and achieving the MBE. I wish him all the best with the book".

-Asif Iqbal MBE BA (Hons), President of Harrow and Brent United Deaf Club

Acknowledgment

I'd like to thank my wife, daughters, and family, especially my father (greatest mentor) and famous inspiration.

Thank you very much to Rachael Veazey RSLI for translating my story from BSL (British Sign Language) into English through a series of voice recordings.

I'm grateful to all hired ghost writers who helped me communicate my message.

CONTENTS

Born Deaf to an MBE i

Dedication iii

Testimonials iv

Acknowledgment vii

About the Author ix

Preface xii

Chapter 1: My Childhood 1

Chapter 2: The School Years 10

Chapter 3: Surviving Secondary School 23

Chapter 4: There are Two Sides to a Coin 34

Chapter 5: The Change in Times 47

Chapter 6: The Communication Barrier 62

Chapter 7: Deaf Business Services LTD 76

Chapter 8: No Experience in Diversity Business ... 90

Chapter 9: The Day of the MBE 101

Chapter 10: The Hustle Never Ends 108

About the Author

Shezad Nawab MBE is a profoundly deaf entrepreneur. His father was from Malawi, his mother was from Pakistan, and his grandfather was from India. However, Shezad was born and raised in Birmingham, United Kingdom.

He has received several awards, including;

- Ummul Mu'minin Khadijah Award for Excellence in Enterprise, 2018.
- Alumni of the Year 2017 in the field of Enterprise and Innovation.
- Member of the Order of the British Empire (MBE) in the New Year 2017 Honours list for services to business and diversity.
- Shortlisted for Young Achiever of the Year, 2016.
- He is listed in the top 10 Most Influential Disabled People in Business, 2014.
- Business Initiative Award, 2011.
- Young Entrepreneur Award, 2011.
- Innovation Voucher Winner, 2010.

He is a specialist in management consulting (from business ideas to scale up), interim executive director; C-level, Chairman, Non-Executive / Board Level Director (risk, performance, strategy, and people), and also an international speaker (business presentations;

training sessions, conferences, keynote speaker, seminars and workshops).

He has been actively supporting several start-ups over the last 17 years and working with SMEs to help them grow their businesses. He benefits from his fluency in six different sign languages – British, American, Arab, South African, Moroccan, and International. Shezad Nawab promotes diversity and encourages it in the business world.

Preface

Each individual has a purpose set in life; for Shezad Nawab, his purpose had been set in stone since birth.

Shezad's book, *Born Deaf To An MBE*, acts as inspiration for every differently-abled individual who desires to be successful in a field of their choice. His experience enlightens the reader by shedding light on the strength of the human mind and how every entrepreneur can unlock the power of their mind by focusing on seasoning their skills, believing in their business and capabilities.

Shezad Nawab's journey from accepting himself the way he had always been to use his diversity to benefit his business community and create deaf awareness in a hearing world is touching. This book acts as evidence that one can achieve their dreams despite the obstacles in their path if one has the right action plan, a manifesto for entrepreneurs and organisations that encourage them to use their diversity to their advantage by highlighting it as their unique selling point.

Born Deaf to an MBE is a step forward for pro-diversity entrepreneurs who encourage the involvement of differently-abled individuals from various ethnicities to bring innovation to the business world. Through this book, many entrepreneurs can learn to establish their footing in the market and help other like-minded individuals succeed. Shezad Nawab aimed to help the deaf community through his passion, entrepreneurship in international business markets, by merging differently-abled but capable individuals in the hearing world of business to improve their chances of equal opportunities. Not only has Shezad accomplished his goal through this book, but he has enabled several up-and-coming entrepreneurs to find their calling.

'Success knows no boundaries'

Why dwell on all that you can't do when there's a whole world out there for you to explore? All you have to do is make the first move to overcome whatever perceived limitations your disability brings you.

Walk with me as I take you on my journey from being born profoundly deaf to becoming an MBE.

Chapter 1

My Childhood

"Being different is not a curse, but a blessing, as it allows you to see the world in a different light."

Difference is a point of dissimilarity between you and any number of people. Some people spend their lives trying to separate themselves from the rest of the people as they strive for uniqueness. Some people spend their lives trying to be like everyone else. I was born different.

Being different isn't a characteristic that should be frowned upon. In fact, we should celebrate being different as it enables you to become intensely creative and view the world from your own unique perspective, which provides you with fresh ideas and the willpower to execute them. However, it is never easy to embrace your differences in a world that teaches its inhabitants to be exhaustingly similar to each other. You have to be strong and keep trying.

I am Shezad Nawab, MBE, and I would like to take you on a journey to relive my past and show you my world that thrives on silence and success.

SHEZAD NAWAB

I was born in Acocks Green, a suburb of Birmingham, in a large family surrounded by people who loved me. We lived in a little terrace house and didn't mind the small space even though both my grandparents and three of my uncles lived with us. My family was very communicative; they expressed how they felt and held long, open discussions over the dinner table. They were the kind of people who loved to talk about their day and listen to the other person talk about theirs. The house was always radiating with chatter and noise, or so I believe, for I don't actually know as I had been born profoundly deaf.

I have extraordinary memories from that house, but all of them are devoid of sound. However, that just makes the pictures in my head much more beautiful. Can you imagine a world where you couldn't hear anything, and everything was always simply silent? Perhaps if you could, you would see the difference in the attention you paid to the little things. I grew up observing my surroundings and cherishing their beauty despite never knowing what the people around me sounded like or what anything sounded like really.

Whether it was the splatter of rain against the cemented street, the blast of glass shattering into a million little pieces, or the sound of my mother's laughter, I will never know what it feels like to be able to hear these sounds and appreciate them. Still, even as a child, I had learned to pay attention to extra details; I had learned to observe and become a participant in my family's expressive nature.

We were a big family, and everyone enjoyed each other's company. Ever since I had gained my senses, I had known that I was different from the rest of my family. I would try to read their lips or guess what they were saying from their expressions. Still, even if I had gotten it right, I wouldn't be satisfied because I have always been the person who needs to see the complete picture to understand it. I don't think there's anything wrong with that because that's how it should be. But it was harder for me because I couldn't hear my parents appreciate me or my grandparents sing lullabies for me. All I could do was feel how strong their love was for me and how hard they tried to communicate with me despite the massive communication barriers between us.

I had been the first deaf child in the family. Hence neither my parents nor my grandparents had any experience in raising a child with hearing disabilities. They didn't know how to communicate in sign language, and I obviously couldn't hear or speak with them, which meant that I had to try harder to learn the simplest things. The love I received from my family made it ten folds easier for me, but it was still harder than anything I've ever done. Your family is the one social institution that consists of a few people who are inherently similar to you. Even if they don't think or behave like you, they are people you can relate to. For me, I didn't have anyone who could relate to facing the same struggles as I did every day of my life, so that made me feel very alone as a child.

Luckily, the biggest perk of being the youngest member of a large family is the constant care and attention you are provided. While my mother was a housewife and used to be extremely busy with housework and chores all day, and my father was an accountant who would work all day to support us, my grandparents were the ones who took care of me, especially my grandfather.

He was rather protective of me, and I enjoyed it because it helped me feel cherished and loved because that showed he cared about me. Even as an infant, I was very close to him as he was to me. My cousins would come over to play with me, as I was just a little baby then, but my grandfather would tell them to come back later as he was taking care of me and didn't want them to disturb me.

I have very fond memories of my grandfather and the love he gave to me. I believe he built the foundation of a successful entrepreneur within me from the day I was born. In addition, he instilled within me a great deal of confidence, care, and the capability to feel empathy I could have been a very confused toddler due to my hearing disability. Still, the care my grandparents bestowed upon me enabled me to move forward without any insecurity holding me back. While I came face to face with a few differences I had to accept about myself later on in life, my grandfather gave me the strength to be confident despite my disability. Because what is there to be ashamed of? What is there to be upset about? How can you be any less of a person just because you have another problem holding you back? Doesn't that make you stronger than the rest of the people because you have it harder than they do?

It took me a long time to accept that a lot of predicaments that I had faced weren't my fault but rather the result of being deaf and that I had moved past them with great flexibility because of the love that I had received from my family initially.

Although I was a toddler and barely understood anything, I understood what love and care felt like, which brings me to note that my early childhood was remarkable because of the people I spent it with. I felt pretty distracted from my problems because I was always playing with one person or another. After all, there were so many people at home.

However, my father decided to move out of Acocks Green and begin a new life in Kidderminster when I was three. I can recall my last memory of Acocks Green, and it was the long road before us as we had set out to leave. It had an expanse of greenery on both sides, with tall leafy trees providing shade to the flowers beneath them. I remember crossing several lorry drivers on the way out and becoming absolutely fascinated with their structure and appearance.

The first few days we arrived in Kidderminster were quite

upsetting for me; it felt like life had dropped us into a new environment where it was just my parents and me. I felt like I had been separated from the rest of my family, and I indeed fought the change for it bored me. But Kidderminster was where our lives began to change, and my family set out on a new path towards success.

My father started a business out of a small shop to sell newspapers and sweets. It was a complicated business to run. But, since we lived above the shop, we spent our days and nights helping my father grow his business. It was a hard time for all of us. My father had begun a new venture and was working very hard to bring it to fruition; my mother had to be an all-rounder as she worked with us and managed to ensure that we were well cared for while I battled with the sudden sense of loneliness that the move had thrust upon me.

On the other hand, moving to Kidderminster grew the relationship that I shared with my parents. Before, my grandparents would take care of me, and now I had more time to spend with my parents to get to know them and understand that they loved me.

I admired the relationship my parents shared; they were not just husband and wife but partners as well. Their friendship always made me wonder how they had managed to become friends after being married. My father was from Malawi while my mother was from Pakistan, and they met after my father's sister got married and moved to Pakistan, where she met my mother and suggested a possible match between her and my father. My grandparents flew to Pakistan to meet my mother. After both families had approved, my parents married and shifted to Birmingham in the UK, where I was born.

My father was very strict. He was the primary provider for our family, and he also supported members of our community. On the other hand, my mother was a housewife. She would stay home and care for my siblings and me once they had been born.

My parents were very open-minded; they would have very open discussions and brilliant conversations every day. But I was deaf, so I couldn't be an active part of every conversation even though they tried their best to include me as well. My parents never really used sign language until I was ten, after which they decided to take level one British Sign Language (BSL) classes to be able to communicate with me better, so before that, we had developed our own version of sign language like a mime or a mixture of gestures that we used to communicate at home. It was our language, and every gesture meant more to me than anyone could ever understand.

Soon, the time to enrol me in school had come, and I remember feeling happy during that part of my life because it was devoid of any problem or predicament. My primary school was a mainstream school, which meant that it had both hearing and deaf students, but I had been enrolled in a specific deaf unit, a place where you went for additional support.

I remember making great friends with whom I spent all my days in primary school. I would still recognise them if I saw them because I have plenty of photographs from my childhood. I would say that primary school was a phase in my life when I fit in the most with the rest of the children my age. Perhaps, it was because children of that age don't use any other means of communication but their heart, which is why I felt the most connected with kids my age then.

A year or two after moving to Kidderminster, my father decided to sell his existing business for a profit as it had become very successful and move to Solihull, which meant that I had to leave my current lifestyle and embrace a massive change once again. I was upset at first, but I have always been a very optimistic person to begin with, so my doubt was soon replaced with a great deal of excitement and curiosity regarding what the next chapter of my life would bring.

I had to leave my old friends behind, but I had new friends to play with after my siblings were born. I have two siblings, one brother who's the middle child and a sister who is the youngest. They are both opposites, and I am somewhere in the middle. While my brother is more of an observer, my sister is an extrovert who loves going out and having fun. I always bonded better with my sister because she had the same sense of confidence that I carried. To be honest, she made everyone around her laugh, and soon she had become the light of all our lives.

Despite struggling with a significant problem at such a young age, I knew what it meant to be happy. I spent my time enjoying the happiness I felt being around my family.

Chapter 2

The School Years

Who defines what "normal" is?

I was always different. Still, I spent my adolescence the way every other kid did, but with a little more struggle and a lot more hustle.

Personally, I think the word 'normal' should be removed from the dictionary because, at the end of the day, we're all different. And, there's nothing wrong with that. But, despite our differences, we as human beings possess the extraordinary capability of coexisting peacefully together. Now, many people put a great deal of effort into making everyone feel at ease. And then, there are others who lack the empathy to understand people with different abilities, features, and beliefs than them.

I have had both kinds of people in my acquaintanceship and, I have to say, we would all become successful ten times faster than usual if we could work together by putting our differences aside or, even better, using our differences as our strengths. Each individual has their own perspective, skills, and qualities. Imagine the massive change that could be brought if we chose to amalgamate all of our qualities, skills, and ideas together to bring reform in the most important social institutions such as business, economy, and education.

When I was younger, I really wished there were better opportunities in the education sector for people like me who suffered from hearing disabilities. I never went to a deaf school; my parents didn't want to put me in one because it was relatively far from my residence in Solihull, and it would have been a long commute every day. They wanted to keep me close to them. However, sometimes I feel like the primary reason why my parents refused to put me in deaf school was that they wanted to test me to see how I would perform in a fast-paced educational environment with other hearing and deaf kids. Perhaps, they didn't wish to limit me.

When we shifted to Solihull, I was about five years old. It was an exciting city with regard to education, business, and entertainment. It had been a step up from Kidderminster, and I was especially eager for this move as it was a positive change we all needed as a family. An improved environment always leads to better living standards, and that increases your mental and physical well-being. I could see an improvement in our lives, and perhaps it was because business was going well. It was time for me to start school and begin a new chapter in my life.

SHEZAD NAWAB

When my parents began searching for the right school for me, they decided to take me with them as they understood I was the one who was going to spend a significant sum of years in whichever school we chose. So, it had to be the right choice, and it had to be mine. We visited many schools. My parents drove me to the best schools all over the city, where I took tours of the campus, met the teachers, principals, and had the chance to witness what the behaviour of other students was like and whether I could conform to that sort of social culture or not.

After a few tiring weeks, one day, my father came home and took out a blackboard. Since we couldn't speak to each other, and my parents hadn't learned sign language yet, it was easier to communicate through a blackboard. Especially when the conversation was as important as the one we were about to have then. I remember he drew large columns on the board and wrote all of the names of the schools I had visited above the columns with their pros and cons listed. I recollect feeling quite uplifted that my father considered my feelings equal to his and my mother's. He had taken note of every advantage and disadvantage I would have if I attended a particular school. He wrote down factors such as the quality of education, student behaviour, and level of efficiency in the deaf support unit, etc. I was only five, and yet I understood everything he meant to tell me because he tried his best to communicate with me in a way that would enable me to really think clearly, and decide which school was best for me.

I decided to attend Windy Arbor Primary School. It was closer than the rest, so I decided to give it a shot. My parents were very happy with my choice, even though they were worried about how I would cope with the rest of the class. But that's not what I was thinking. I was busy imagining the great times I would have in school, all the friends I'd make, and the memories we would create. I was always a very creative child, and in my mind's eye, being able to go to school was like a new fun activity. Perhaps, my eagerness, motivation, and passion to attain an education were the factors that enabled me to stay confident despite my disability.

Windy Arbor was a small primary school with only one building where we would study on the first floor. There was an apt deaf support unit, but I was happy that they had a little playground where all of the kids could play together. I enjoyed going to school. I liked studying and returning to my parents, who would support, cherish, and shower me with pride. The first few months were beautiful, and I had the best time. I will never forget any of it because it was one of the most incredible times of my life. The happiness that you feel when you're a child is comparatively more overwhelming and powerful, which is why I keep this particular memory close to my heart.

However, Windy Arbor Primary School had small classrooms.

There was less space to move around and explore. I believe it is crucial to have ample, colourful space as a classroom to maintain a child's attention. The teachers were always busy. I had so many questions, but not all of them were answered. It became difficult to keep up as the teacher spoke while she wrote on the board, and other kids could hear her as they noted what she was saying. But I couldn't hear the teacher, nor could I lip-read and write simultaneously. All of it was new to me, like it was to every other kid in class, but they had a competitive advantage that I naturally didn't. The other students in my class were quite clever, now that I think of it. As a result, I started feeling less qualified. Therefore, I took support from the deaf unit that provided me with a communication support worker (CSW) who would help me communicate with the teacher in class, take notes, and prepare for exams.

It was a challenging time, but I made the most of it. I would play with all of the children, who knew me as the deaf kid, and they were all very nice to me. Back in primary school, your colour, race, language, or abilities didn't interfere with the friendships and bonds you created because children that young don't really care about all of that. Children care about love, respect, and having a good time together. Isn't that what truly matters? Well, it should. Even though I was the only Muslim Asian student in the class, and all of the other kids were white, I was very confident and friendly, which helped me make tons of friends that I have very fond memories with. I don't remember their names, but I might be able to recognise someone if I see them again because I can never forget the magnificent memories we made in primary school.

On the other hand, Windy Arbor Primary School didn't have a second division, and as much as I distracted myself, I was lagging behind. The deaf unit they had wasn't as efficient as the other schools, and I wasn't getting the proper attention and support I needed. There was no room to grow, and I knew that to make better progress, I would have to shift to another school with a better capability to support me and meet my needs as a deaf child. My parents wanted me to improve, so they decided that a change was mandatory and admitted me to Peterbrook Primary School.

I loved Peterbrook Primary School. It was much bigger than Windy Arbor, and it had bigger classrooms, two floors, and a secondary division as well. There were more students in Peterbrook, which meant that I had even more friends to play with. There were two beautiful buildings, one was dedicated to the primary sector, and the other was for the secondary sector. I benefitted from the fact that Peterbrook had different classrooms for the fifth and seventh years, so it was like a mental progression along with a physical one. The teachers were quite smart at Peterbrook, and I had more support in academics than I had in Windy Arbor.

Nevertheless, my struggles didn't simply disappear. As I got older and progressed from one year to the next, keeping up with my academics became problematic as the material itself increased in difficulty. While I had support from a communication social worker, studying itself had become strenuous and tough. Exams were specifically tough; I would get three hours to finish an exam while other kids would only get two hours to get complete their exam. I was grateful for the extra help, but assistance didn't decrease the difficulty, complications, and confusion that I was facing; it simply enabled me to cope with it.

After all, I was a profoundly deaf person who was attending a mainstream school with a large majority of hearing children. I felt different. All of them communicated verbally. While there were more teachers at Peterbrook than at Windy Arbor, they still didn't have the time to sit me down and explain every little thing to me. I'd ask my communication support worker (CSW), but I couldn't understand because we had a language difference. I needed a lot of support. Everything needed to be broken down for me.

For the longest time, I blamed myself for not being smart enough. But I later realised that it wasn't my fault; I was just deaf. The children who attended Peterbrook were quick to read because they knew what the words would sound like, while I didn't. I couldn't understand a lot of things, and even as a child, I was deeply interested in the meaning behind every word in every sentence. People would have to draw pictures for me to understand and see what I had been missing out on. Other kids would get two hours to finish an exam, while I would get three to complete one because the examination system was created by hearing people for other people who can hear. I always needed additional support, specifically to fulfil my language and communication needs.

Times had changed, and so had the students that I had grown up with in school. Communication is key to a successful friendship, and I couldn't communicate with the rest of the kids I knew. I often felt lonely and began to believe that I didn't fit in with everyone else. There were other students who suffered from disabilities such as dyslexia, but I could only see my own struggle and how different it was from the rest. Then, I made two friends — Jonathan Lister and Jay Thomas-Morton. They were both deaf boys who became great friends with me, understood me and my problems, and chose to stay by my side throughout the years that followed. When they weren't around, I could sense myself slipping into depression, and that is when I would ask myself: why had my parents let me go to a mainstream school when they knew how difficult it would be for me? I thought about it for a long time, and then I came up with the answer: my parents believed in me.

My parents were preparing me for the real world, where I would have interactions with all kinds of people. They wanted me to meet people with disabilities, people who didn't have any problems whatsoever, people who would support me, and people who would try to hold me back. In the grand scheme of things, despite mainstream education is difficult to achieve for me due to my hearing disability, I feel quite lucky to have been through that phase of my life successfully. I wouldn't have been able to do that had I been refrained by my parents in an effort not to let me step out of their comfort zone.

    I attended mainstream schools all my life, but my parents always chose schools with a proper deaf support unit in case I were to encounter any difficulties. While my parents pushed me out of my comfort zone, they also tried to reign me in at the same time because they were worried about my capability to become successful given my disability. Still, they never seized to believe in me, and their belief is what enabled me to ease through the most painful parts of my life with nothing but a few scars and plenty of success to look behind at.

    Don't get me wrong. I'm not saying it was easy; it was actually quite hard. I think the most difficult phase of my life was between my teens and when I went to college because it was actually very hard to move ahead in life with my disability holding me back. It took a long time for me to free myself of the burden that society placed on me for being different. Still, I was only able to do that because I had always naturally been a confident person. I had been lucky to have a significant number of supporters at home and in other areas of life, so it was easier for me to rid myself of societal stigma. However, it isn't as easy for other people like me, which is why I want this book to be a source of inspiration for them, a glimmer of hope. I want everyone, whether they suffer from disabilities or not, to know that there is always a way out of despair and difficulty; you simply mustn't give up. I didn't give up.

If you give up, you lose your chance to do better and trust me when I say you can always do better. There is no cap on human improvement, and your disabilities or problems only derail you from achieving success. It is always better to keep fighting because when you finally get to where you want to be, it will mean more to you since you worked your way to get there. I speak from experience when I say that your success will bring you tenfold more joy if you overcome many obstacles to achieve it.

People often underestimate the strength it takes to survive. I'm not doing that. I am telling you that you have to keep surviving and keep fighting. One day, you will transform your dreams into reality. I did, too, despite the obstacles, I constantly stumbled upon. I became successful when I turned those very obstacles into steppingstones on the ladder to success. I reached my destination in no time once I figured out how to continuously believe in myself and my work.

Your definition of success has great significance, as knowing what you want out of life is the first step towards getting it. When I was younger, I wanted to be heard, not by my words but through the sound of my success. I wanted to hear it too. At the back of my mind, I always knew what I wanted to do, and that helped me work harder and smarter with increased levels of motivation that enabled me to reach a new high I hadn't even anticipated before then.

Prior to the age of ten, I accompanied my father to meet clients, and I paid great attention to how he would conduct meetings or carry a conversation. He would show clients around various properties and reveal different parts of them in such an exciting manner. There was passion in his body language and certainty in his eyes. He would give his clients extensive tours around the entire property, such as the kitchen, living room, bedrooms, etc.

If a particular property or a part of it were to be renovated, I watched him plan and execute the renovation flawlessly. I've witnessed the transformation of entire buildings that he would buy, renovate, and then sell for a substantial profit. Organisation was crucial to him. He had activity lists for every day with the meetings he had to conduct, the legal advice he needed to take, and other appointments. In fact, his entire year would be scheduled and planned, which taught me a lot about the power of organisation and how profoundly it can benefit you. I spent a long time observing my father, and I was impressed beyond measure by the quality of his work and the success that he attained through it.

My father made success look easy to attain, and I thought that if I tried hard enough, I could be successful just like him. I was inspired by his mindset, planning, and ability to maintain a work-life balance. Even the little things he did were a source of motivation for me. My father was a property developer. While I observed him become the best role model any child could have, I decided that I wanted to work in investment property too. It was the best decision of my life because it had been rooted in passion and inspiration.

I had a great childhood. Despite being deaf, I heard the love and respect that people gave to me because to really hear and understand someone; you don't need to physically be able to hear them. Instead, what you do need is to feel their pride, hurt, and love. Actions speak louder than words, and I am its biggest witness. There have been so many instances when I couldn't understand what my parents would be saying, but I would know what they meant. Not simply because I had observed their body language for a long time but because I had learned more about their feelings and how they would portray them.

My family travelled a lot, and I enjoyed the experience thoroughly. We once flew to Florida. At first, I didn't know what we were going there for, but when I witnessed my father's excitement, I understood that he had bought another property. He looked absolutely fascinated as he spoke about the difference in property law in the United States of America and the UK. He had spent that entire afternoon figuring out how to make adjustments with the property laws that are used in the US. He wanted to learn more about every country, city, or state he went to so he could incorporate that knowledge into his business.

I remember when my family travelled to Morocco. I recall how excited my father had been. He had said that factors such as language, etiquette, and culture all affected business. For example, private limited companies are called SARL in Morocco, which is a French word, and he had tried to explain to me how something as little as a word can make all the difference in the world. Sometime later, when I expanded my own business to Morocco, I understood what he had meant all those years ago.

I was about ten years old when I told my father that I wanted to be rich. I wanted to be like him. But, instead of telling me that I wouldn't be able to do it because I was deaf, he nodded at me and told me that it would take a lot of hard work. Then, he proceeded to ask me if I was ready for it. I remember nodding profusely with growing anticipation for what he was about to say next, and then he invited me to join him for work from the next day where I could work in the back office to get to know the employees, the people I would be working with, the business, and find out whether I was actually ready for it.

Little did he know, I was born ready.

Chapter 3

Surviving Secondary School

Imagine being trapped inside of a transparent soundproof box. Now, try to visualise yourself trapped within that clear soundproof box while you sit in a classroom with many other hearing students and a teacher you cannot hear but have to learn from anyway. At this point, you will realise the only way you learn is if you gather information visually since you cannot hear anything. You can either rely on lip-reading, concentrating on the teacher's body language, or simply understanding by reading what they've written on the board.

You may feel upset because no other student, but you are trapped within a box devoid of any sound and that, too, in a classroom. You would be tested on what you've learned or were supposed to learn. Surprisingly, you are tested in the same manner as other children, even though you haven't learned the same way they have in the classroom. Then, your score on any test or exam would be compared to the rest of the students. It seems a bit unfair, doesn't it?

Well, that's how I had begun to feel as I grew up.

When you're younger, you possess a stronger will to keep

going despite all of the challenges that you may face because you are unaware of the magnitude of your troubles. Your innocence enables you to move forward without becoming overwhelmed, and that is how I kept moving ahead as I overcame every obstacle I faced in mainstream primary and middle schools. Then, I gained admission to Lyndon Secondary School, and I understood what the word "difficult" truly meant.

I had faced several predicaments throughout my early academic years, but I had always managed to overcome them. Perhaps, education itself was easier to understand when I was in primary and middle school. As I progressed to higher education, the problems that I would face as a profoundly deaf teenager became much more real and complicated.

I remember my first day at Lyndon Secondary school. The architecture of the school was quite different from my previous schools. The building itself was much larger than any of my previous schools had been. I recall looking around and feeling fascinated by what I saw because I was so excited to study at a school that could host so many students. Unlike my previous schools that only had one classroom where I spent many years, Lyndon secondary school had many classrooms. While it may not feel like a big difference, but it was a massive change for me as it meant that I had to navigate to a different classroom for every lesson, and that was a little difficult for me, but I enjoyed moving around if I knew where I was supposed to go.

While I was excited to enter a new chapter in my life, I felt increasingly nervous. I didn't know who would walk me to class or how I would get there. I couldn't hear or speak with any of the other students or faculty, so I couldn't simply ask them where to go either. I looked forward to finding someone who could guide me and help me find my way around the expansive school building. I felt thrilled to be attending a school that was different from every other school that I had been to, but that change also brought fear and doubt along with it.

My first class on the first day of school was in the science lab, and when I got there, the first thing that caught my eye was that it had rows and rows of desks. I sat in front, and all of the other students sat behind me. I was the only deaf student in the class, and if that wasn't enough to separate me from the rest of the students, I always sat in front, which meant that I couldn't be a part of all of the fun that went on at the back. I would be busy trying to comprehend what the teacher said by carefully looking at their lips, and, thankfully, I also had the help of a communication support worker (CSW). The rest of the students were quite lively; some were even quite naughty. Even though I was the only Asian student in the class and profoundly deaf, the other students were quite empathic. I enjoyed the environment that we had in class quite thoroughly.

There was one phase of my school life that I will never fail to forget. It all began when I progressed to the ninth year, and the teachers started mentally preparing the students for GCSE's that would commence in year eleven. The students were petrified, and there was a thick tension in the atmosphere. The teachers then attempted to relieve the students by informing us that we would start preparing for GCSE's in year ten.

I don't remember being able to relax for a single moment afterwards.

I started preparing for my GCSE's in the tenth year, which was a year before I was supposed to sit for the actual exams. The school prepared us for the GCSE's through mock examinations and several tests. That's when the stress began to get to me. However, when I started year eleven, academics became far more complicated than they ever had been before. If there is one subject that I found great difficulty progressing in, it was English. There was a huge difference between spoken and written English and British Sign Language (BSL). The teachers would ask me tough questions, which involved complicated jargon that confused me. It was a very strenuous time for me, and with every passing day, I began to feel increasingly exhausted.

Years ten and eleven were challenging, academically and

emotionally; I struggled with the exams. I was confused and nervous throughout. Although I was confident, I kept rechecking my exams even after I had finished them. Even if I felt like I did well on my tests, it would be difficult for the other person to understand what I had written due to the difference in written English and British Sign Language (BSL).

The hearing students gave their exams in another hall room dedicated solely for that purpose. I would sit in a separate room on my own with only one table and a single interpreter who would sometimes translate what the questions meant in sign language. My interpreter, who was also my communication support worker (CSW), would first explain the exam to me in sign language. I would then solve the question paper in British English. It was complicated when our exams had multiple-choice questions, which would have four options. I would have a very difficult time picking one option over the other as I had to make up my mind within a short amount of time. I was already perplexed about everything towards the end of secondary school, and I believe that GCSE's pushed me off the edge.

One thing that helped me was that I received extra time to finish my exams. While other students were given two hours to finish an exam, I could finish the exam in three hours. I was grateful for the opportunities that I had, but they made me feel all the more different than the rest of the children.

Perhaps, not having that many close friends made my high school experience worse. It wasn't like I didn't try to make more friends. I was incredibly social. When we arrived at school in the morning, we needed to visit the registration room to mark our attendance, which was taken twice daily. I would know all of the students in the registration room; that's how much I enjoyed getting to know people. Sometimes after class, I went into different rooms dedicated to different programmes such as IT or Math, for example, and I would hang out with people I knew from that class. However, although I knew many people, I just knew them by their faces and not even by their names.

Despite every problem I was forced to conquer to keep moving forward, now that I look back, I truly feel as if high school is the most exciting time in everyone's lives. It is when you are one decision away from a completely different future. Every decision you make during your years in high school impacts your future in unforeseeable ways. When you're in secondary school, everyone finds a career for themselves they feel would suit them in the future. So when my communication support worker (CSW) asked me what I wanted to be in the future, I said I wanted to be a pilot.

To my surprise, she made some calls and then took me to visit Alpha Flight Services. We simply looked around at first, and I found that I liked the office as in the workspace, the work environment, and the people who worked there. Then, thanks to the law of attraction and its powerful methods of connecting you with everything you truly desire, I got selected as one of the internees for Alpha Flight Services.

I believe I was about fifteen when I started working at Alpha Flight Services. I was first trained, and then after my GCSE's, I started working for a wage but only at a starting position in food and production preparation. The position I was working at didn't matter to my family or me. The fact that I was working to build financial stability within myself made me and my family quite happy. My parents were delighted that I had a work placement and then a paying job because it was an excellent start for a teenager. Both of my parents once visited my school and met my teachers, who praised me and said that there were students who worked better than me. However, there was one thing that my parents were proud of, and that was my work ethic, which was quite improved from the rest of the students. I wanted to work and earn money with a passion that was so strong that it fuelled my entire career.

I would work for four days consecutively and then be awarded two days off. On the four days that I worked, I woke up at six, put on my uniform. I specifically remember not being allowed to wear any accessories to work or even carrying a mobile around during my shift. I would start working by seven AM, and I would continue working till seven PM in the evening as it was a twelve-hour shift with a few breaks in between. I'd have my lunch break by eleven or twelve PM when I could use my mobile and have lunch. Work was particularly intense when the airport was especially crowded due to many ongoing flights. Otherwise, it was plain boring.

When I received my results for the GCSE's, I was working at Birmingham airport. My mother picked up the result and brought it home. When I got back from work and opened the result sheet, I felt my heart shatter because I realised that I had gotten a very low grade. The results weren't exactly horrendous or disappointing, but I was upset about them because I had tried hard to get a good grade despite everything that stood in my way. The best grade I had gotten was a C in art, which meant a lot to me. However, I realised I needed extra support if I wanted to go to college, which I knew I needed to because even though several problems were standing in my way, I believed that I could move past them.

My parents were worried about my future, so they sat with me one night and told me that one option for overcoming my problems was to have a cochlear implant. So, I tried it. I visited a testing centre at the age of twelve and then had a cochlear implant at age thirteen. It was certainly a very enlightening experience.

I could suddenly hear every kind of sound, and I was surprised that there were so many. I could hear the traffic, which was so loud, the wind as it tickled my ear and the sound of leaves rustling as I ran past them on a chilly night. I was fascinated. I even tried speech therapy to make good use of my cochlear implant as I had it for some time in secondary school, but not for long.

I had to learn what different things sounded like, and as easy as that may sound, it wasn't. I had to keep going to the testing centre to get the sound levels in my cochlear checked and adjusted. Still, it was so painful that I asked the doctors why it hurt so much, and they told me that my cochlear implant was affecting the nerve endings in my face every time they switched it because it would pull my cheeks, which would then put me through a great deal of pain.

Nevertheless, I persevered in learning. Then, I went to Derby College for Deaf People (DCDP), a proper institution for the deaf. I attended that college for three months. The deaf community at DCDP was so strong, and everyone used sign language, I had a cochlear implant, but their authenticity was so inspiring that I chose to use sign language. But then, I noticed that people at college had begun to bully me, and at first, I couldn't understand why. I thought I was a good person, I do well academically, and I come across as reasonably confident, so why are they bullying me?

I had never experienced bullying before, so I couldn't understand why it was happening then. Still, now that I think about it, I understand it was because the deaf community was so sensitive to technology and the changes it brought to their life. Every other student at DCDP was deaf, and I was the only cochlear user at the university at the time. I was worried about not completing my education at DCDP because of the negative impact that the bullying was having on me. I thought I wouldn't be able to go on with the degree of distress the bullying thrust upon me, so I chose to go back to Birmingham, which I don't regret.

I didn't miss it, but I will always remember DCDP. The college itself wasn't great. Still, the deaf community left such an everlasting impression on me that I decided I didn't need a cochlear implant because sign language is very powerful on its own. It's the most powerful language in the world because it is relayed through the heart. I felt quite different when I had my cochlear implant when I could hear everything; everything felt different. But I had to let it go. The pain I was suffering, as a result, wasn't worth the trouble.

I stopped using the cochlear implant at the age of eighteen.

When I had the cochlear implant, I could have conversations with everyone else, but I was still heavily reliant on sign language. My parents noticed how badly the cochlear implant had affected me, and my siblings had begun to feel like I had changed. They tried to help me move past all of my problems. My family understood that the cochlear implant had only helped me hear environmental sounds, which wasn't exactly that helpful in practical life.

All that mattered was that I wanted to be myself. I was so

grateful that everyone understood that I chose to be a deaf person who could use sign language instead of being someone who isn't even a hearing person but an individual who can hear some sounds but has to suffer so much pain for it. I will always be thankful to my family for their support, as not everyone would have been able to accept or respect my wishes, but my parents and siblings continued forever.

Chapter 4

There are Two Sides to a Coin

College life is recognised as one of the most exceptional years of one's development. It is entirely different from school life. College life involves new experiences and introduces us to situations that we were not familiar with earlier. For some people, college life suggests savouring life to the fullest. While for others, it is a reminder to become earnest about their career and study thoroughly for a more favourable future.

Nevertheless, the time we spent at college remains a memorable period for all of us. I believe that people who can attain an education should be grateful as everyone isn't lucky enough to experience college life. People do not get the chance to go to college due to various reasons. At times, it is because they do not have a solid financial background to do so. In contradiction, other times, they have other responsibilities to fulfil. Many people who have experienced college life always wish to turn back time to live it all again.

College life is a big transition from school life. Change is expected in an individual who goes to college. When they walk out of college with their respective degrees, they are different from those who walked in. Our schools are a safe place where we grow up and spend half our lives. The transition to college is so sudden that you're no longer protected by your school time's teachers and friends.

College life is massively different when compared to school; it's a new experience. In school, you have bells that sound the ending of a class, and students must wear uniforms. There are strict timetables to be followed. I found college to be much more flexible in terms of what you could and could not do. You can go to the library to study on your own time. There wasn't as much tutor input in college as there was in school. It was just generally better.

College life presents a lot of challenges for you. I am profoundly deaf, and I have witnessed perfectly abled students struggle to keep up with college. I was attending a college full of unfamiliar faces who I needed to mingle with; this taught me the importance of socialising and forming opinions of my own. In college, I learned how to use my free will and become more confident and composed.

Throughout school life, we are unconsciously dependent on our friends and/or teachers. College life, however, teaches us to be independent. It makes us stronger and teaches us to fight our own battles. College developed insight within me and provided clarity about the kind of professional life I wanted to lead. We progress to decisions that affect our future all by ourselves, as in school life, our parents did it for us.

Additionally, in schools, we viewed our teachers as our mentors and sometimes even parents. We regarded them with respect and kept a safe distance. However, in college life, the teacher-student relationship becomes more casual. They become more or less like our friends, and we share our troubles and happiness with them. Every college I went to, my mentors always secured a special place in my heart.

However, college life is different for everyone. While many individuals have wonderful college experiences, some don't. I went to four colleges, and I have several memories that were both advantageous and disadvantageous for me.

I went to Derby College for The Deaf (DCDP) when I was sixteen, and then I kept moving from one college to the next to find the right one for me. The colleges that I attended next were Bournville College, Redditch college (former of North East Worcestershire; NEW college), and Solihull college (former of Solihull College of Technology).

I went to four different colleges, and I am proud of myself for never settling for any less than what I deserved. My parents always supported me in my journey to find the right college for myself, and that played a significant part in moving from one college to the next without hesitation. In today's world, many people do not have the chance to make a different choice than what is available to them because they do not have other options. They are held back by personal reservations that they either do not deserve better or are fine. It is uncommon for students to keep moving from one college to the next because they are bound by circumstances, family expectations, and the idea that it is not justified to keep looking until you find the right one.

I firmly believe that no one should settle for less than what they deserve because every individual has a unique gift to offer that should not be overlooked. I never gave up. And in the end, it paid off. I found the right college for myself and spent several years there with great contentment embedded in my heart. Compromising your education can never be an option.

My experience at Derby College for Deaf People (DCDP) wasn't pleasant. I regret going to DCDP because I was bullied there for the first time in my entire life. Before attending DCDP, I had thought that going to DCDP would be a more sensible choice as it was a college, especially for the deaf, and I am a profoundly deaf person. So, acceptance from the rest of the student body wouldn't be an issue. Despite all that, I had to endure bullying instead.

Students at DCDP were very focused on sign language, and they were very skilled at it. Unfortunately, their love for sign language overshadowed humility. Hence, they became biased. The students at

DCDP hated the idea of cochlear implantation, and I had one, and that put me in a difficult position with the rest of the student body. Moreover, I was glad for the opportunity to leave that college because it wasn't a very professional college, and I was proved right when it closed down a few years after I had left.

I faced many predicaments when I attended other mainstream colleges as well, where most of the student body consisted of hearing individuals and some were deaf. The biggest problem I encountered in mainstream colleges was my inability to socialise to the extent that I wanted. I faced social issues in mainstream colleges because hanging out with the friends I made was quite difficult. We had different timetables, and there was a prominent communication barrier between me and hearing individuals, so it became problematic and immensely strenuous to set meetings with them.

After Derby College for Deaf People (DCDP), I went to Bournville College, where the academic experience was far better, but I still wasn't completely satisfied. Then, I attended Redditch College, which was relatively peaceful, actually too quiet, and I wanted a little more excitement in my life, so I moved on to Solihull College, which thankfully checked all of the boxes on my list.

I felt like all of the colleges that I attended weren't a good fit for me until I came to Solihull College. So out of the four colleges I attended, Solihull was the best college for me because it had high-level academic courses, and my tutors were great. My favourite tutor was James Taylor, and he was fantastic. He had an exceptional experience when it came to teaching, and it showed. There were so many international students at Solihull College, which made my class very diverse. I was still the only deaf student in class, but that never became a problem. I liked it. It was such a brilliant experience.

I have lovely memories of Solihull College. One of my favourites is when the student body would gather to discuss issues students face and how we could all join hands to solve them. I was very interested in having group discussions even though I would be the only deaf person taking part in them. I would have an interpreter sitting opposite me, and they would help me communicate with the rest. The first meeting I ever went to had altered my perception of education because it made me realise what good education was all about. We talked about students, tutors, everything that was happening, etc., and that's when I looked around and realised what a different college it was compared to the rest of the colleges that I had attended.

People often ask me what the best age is to start planning for the future. To be honest, there is no right age to begin working on your future. The sooner, the better.

However, at the critical age of sixteen, before you give your GCSEs, you must think about what the next step will be. Many individuals start preparing for college very early, while some decide that they do not wish to go to college or continue with higher studies. Perhaps, they wish to start working, take part in an apprenticeship or work their way to the top. Evidently, I do not have a preference for which way one should go; that depends solely on the individual, which is why planning and self-reflection are two critical habits that should be practiced skillfully from the beginning of teenage as it leads to profitable decisions in the future.

If I wasn't doing business today, I wonder what I would have been doing. Imagine, if I hadn't received a proper education, I'd have to hone my skills and practice them to increase my efficiency because that would become my unique selling point. Perhaps, I would have been in finance or management, but I would have always wanted to become an entrepreneur because I have witnessed my father practice it for years and what I've come to love as a career.

It took me a long time to find the right college for myself, and that happened after I tried four other colleges. I had to experience the student life at each college to decide which one was the best fit for me, and it took years for me to find the right one and feel comfortable about my choice. That is why planning is such a vital step when making life choices because you really have to figure out the right decision for you before knowing what the outcome will definitely be.

I've always experienced a mainstream education; I've always

been a part of a diverse community consisting of deaf and hearing people. Mainstream schools provide better facilities even though it can be more difficult to blend in a diverse society for a deaf individual. However, it is important to gain better access to excellent resources, especially if you struggle with a disability, as I did. At the end of the day, it's not really about mainstream or deaf schools; it's about which institution can provide you with easy access to all of the resources that you need as an individual student to attain a fulfilling education.

It's essential to remember that the best colleges offer understanding, care, and efficiency. My favourite college out of all of the ones I attended was Solihull College, and that was because they possessed great deaf awareness, shared a special connection with all of their students, and reminded me what excellent education felt like – that's how college should feel.

Along with education, entrepreneurship also meant a lot to me. I had begun planning my future and pondering over who I wanted to be from a very early age. When I was about sixteen, I started saving my wages from my first job. My father was very involved in my life, and he paid close attention to what I did or did not do, so he asked me,

"Why are you saving your wages, son?"

I told him that I had to because I wanted to buy myself

something special to remind me of my first job. He then told me to think about it for a while and then tell him. I did, and after a while, I said I wanted to buy a house. He was quite pleased. He offered to help me, and I accepted right away because I trusted his capability to find me the right house for myself. After a tiring search, I bought a newly built terrace house with 2-3 bedrooms, for £40,000 pounds. Today, it's worth £250,000 pounds. In the beginning, I had thought it was perilous. I was nervous about it as I thought the value would decrease. My lawyer told me not to worry about any of it.

I learned a great deal from my experience of buying that house as it was my first purchase of property, and it proved to be worth a lot more than I bought it for because it had a significant intangible value for me. It taught me patience, sensibility, and risk calculation.

As you can probably tell at this point, I had started working to bring myself to a good position from a very young age. The truth is, I had everything but a partner. I tasted success very early on, but I wanted to be with someone with whom I could celebrate that success. Sometimes, life truly surprises you.

I had never met my wife, and initially, we met through a website called www.deafchat.com. At that time, we didn't have a feature for video calling, and we were just communicating through the website, getting to know each other, just asking for details about each other like our real names, ages, etc. I didn't know how she was in real life even though we chatted for two years, but I had never even seen a photograph of her. I asked for her photo after years.

We were finally able to have a conversation on video call after a long wait, but we didn't have a good internet connection back then, so it was quite frustrating. I knew her family by reputation because my aunt (my mother's sister) used to live in South Africa, and I would continue to ask her questions so she would give me inside information about my wife's family because she knew them well. I finally had the chance to meet her when her parents went to Makkah for Umrah (Pilgrimage), and then on the way back, her family, including all of her nieces and nephews, visited England. I finally had the chance to meet her after two years of purely online interaction. However, my wife used the South African Sign Language (SASL) and American Sign Language (ASL).

In contrast, I used British Sign Language (BSL), which made it very difficult to communicate in our preferred language of the sign because we used different signing systems. Despite all that, we didn't give up on our relationship because it meant a lot to us. Although it may seem odd, we communicated through written text quite often. It worked for us.

Education isn't that great in South Africa. If you're fortunate enough, the most you can do is get a private tutor. That's what my wife had done. She then attended a Gallaudet University in

Washington, DC, United States, but later decided to come back. My wife and I have very different cultures. For example, in South Africa, she was used to employing several servants, especially maids, who would help with all of the housework. But in the UK, we cook, clean, and manage everything ourselves. My wife loves sharing stories about her life, her parents, and her childhood with me, and I love listening to them because she has had a very incredible life that interests me.

However, my favourite story is from the time when I proposed to her. I remember being at my house with my parents, in our vast lush garden. I asked her simple questions because I wanted to get to know the real her. I asked her romantic questions like, what's your favourite colour? What's your favourite food? What are your hobbies? My wife, on the other hand, was very enthusiastic while answering all of my questions.

She was so supportive, writing and signing back answers as quickly as she could, and then I was like, you know what, I want to marry you. Do you want to marry me too? And, very quickly, my wife said yes. We told our parents, and both of our families were happy. I wanted to marry her because she's brilliant and she inspires me. She is a swift learner and never fails to amuse me. She's amazing, and I am so glad that I decided to make her mine that day.

We saw each other for six months; I was working five days a week, but we made it work. Our families got along well with each other, and so did my wife and me. We have very similar personalities, we're both heavily interested in sign language, and we have the same level of intelligence. After spending time with my wife, I told my parents that I thought this was the woman for me, and they agreed because both of our families understood the love that we had for each other. We got engaged, and in six months, we were then married. I flew to her country for the ceremony. The wedding was huge, and I think there were about 1,500 people who attended. It was enormous considering the number of tables and chairs set up.

The guests had been segregated with men on one side and women on the other as my wedding took place in a very strong Muslim community, and my father-in-law is a renowned Islamic leader and runs a very successful business, a company of Demolition Contractor and Atomic Demolishers. My mother-in-law is an amazing woman as well. She has six children, and she cooks for each one of them. All of their children are hearing except for my wife and her brother, who are profoundly deaf.

We got married in Durban in South Africa. The day the celebrations had ended, we left for our honeymoon in Mauritius; I will never forget it. It was so beautiful, and we had such a great time. The weather was perfect, the island was beautiful, and the community there was very different from the communities I had met and lived in before. We thoroughly enjoyed touring the island, swimming in the bright blue sea, going to restaurants three times a day, and just being out and about. I was travelling with my best friend, my wife. It was a new feeling, one I wasn't used to but cherished wholeheartedly.

Before getting married, I would always go on holiday with my parents. Then, I went with my wife. I was so used to them being around, travelling with them, eating with them, and then my parents said, "Get married, son. You're a man now." I felt a very monumental change in my life after getting married because marriage does change a man. You have a new person to get used to as a part of your life; there are new rules that you have to live with and a lifestyle you have to adjust to and remember to enjoy.

My wife and I have been married for a long time now, and we have two hearing daughters. My wife is fantastic, and I still love her as much as I did when I first saw her, if not more; her passion fuels mine. She is very ambitious about cooking, and she's turned it into a little business for herself in which she cooks and sells food produce. I couldn't have chosen a better partner for myself or a better friend.

Chapter 5

The Change in Times

Marriage is a sacred union, which binds man and woman into a promise to do better and be appreciated for that effort.

Immediately after I got married, I felt its overwhelming positivity envelop me in its folds, as it had been a very positive turn of events in my life. I believe that marriage became a prominent factor that drove my success to its completion. If you are married to the right person, they can become your partner and enable you to achieve your dreams without giving up. My wife became my motivator. Every day that we spent together provided me with the strength that I needed to do better in other areas of my life.

We have always shared a profound connection and understanding that enabled our relationship to become our haven. Both of us are profoundly deaf, yet we understood each other like no one else ever has before. We use sign language to communicate. Every sign, symbol, and gesture is equal to the most beautiful of words for us.

I suppose it is safe to say that we get on well. We are not one of those couples who argue or bicker all the time. We communicate, and if there is a problem in front of us, we solve it together. We rarely ever argue. On the other hand, I know couples who argue all the time, and they love each other to the ends of the earth too, that is completely all right, but that's not us. We have a powerful and positive relationship.

I believe that the first few weeks of marriage really set the foundation for a relationship forever. The first few weeks of my marriage were the beginning of endless bliss and affection. How could they not be? We spent the following days after our marriage on one of the most beautiful islands in the world.

When we landed in Mauritius, the scenic beauty was so foreign and overwhelming that we felt a bit of a shock wave penetrate through us. We had just left Africa, and the island that we had arrived in was so different from the city that we had left behind. Everything about Mauritius was different, the culture, food, people, you name it. Mauritius is primarily inhabited by Asian people. They have brought a beautiful mix of their culture, cuisine, and persona to the island. The weather was gorgeous. It rained every other day; then the sun would reveal itself in all its blazing glory and shine down upon us with its fulfilling warmth. Mauritius has a beautiful landscape, architecture, and scenery. In fact, the island blossomed even more and became fresher after the rain. It is a wonderful destination to go to, especially if you are looking for some place romantic!

Our honeymoon was very romantic, indeed. We thoroughly enjoyed every moment. It is vital to know when to let go of everything else and focus your attention on the people who really matter. On my honeymoon, I switched off from family, business, and work. I did not even work through my phone. I completely concentrated on my wonderful wife and spent every minute of our honeymoon indulging in deep, meaningful conversations with her that became the foundation of our relationship. We talked and talked and talked for five days straight. With the time that we had leftover, we went swimming, treated each other to delicious food, and shopped endlessly. We had such a wonderful time.

I will never forget the timeless memories that my wife and I made together.

There was this one time when my wife and I were going for a walk, and we thought we should have a little look at the walkway surrounded by the rocks on the beach. I am a bit of an adventurist and soon found excitement boiling up within me. My wife saw right through me and told me not to go on the rocks because they were slippery, and she just would not stop telling me not to go and step on them even after I told her that I would not, even though that was exactly what I wanted to do. However, I soon realised that she was extra cautious because my mother had already gotten to her. Indeed, my mother had already coached her not to let me do anything crazy and to keep me safe, so that is exactly what she was doing.

Another memory I absolutely cannot get out of my head. One that I often laugh about is when my wife and I were on our honeymoon. We had a hearing tour guide who took us around the island; we did not know what he was saying, though. There were so many people selling food around the island that looked delicious. I obviously knew that it was street food; I did not imagine that it would be any different from the street food I had before. There were freshly cut mangoes, finely diced pineapples, and beautifully peeled pomegranates. When I bought them from the seller, he mixed them up with many spices. I found myself shocked by the spice level and how different the fruit tasted when it was mixed with signature Asian seasonings. While I found it too spicy, my wife found it delicious.

After we returned from our honeymoon, I went back to studying, a very rapid turn to reality.

I was fortunate to have my wife's support as I had made it abundantly clear that my education would always be a priority to me. When I got engaged to my wife, I had shared my plans with her honestly. She already knew my ambitions, and she appreciated them. We lived with my family until I completed my education. She was fine with it. She motivated me even when I was very awfully busy studying. She helped me focus on what truly mattered: our relationship, my ambitions, and mutual success and happiness for both of us.

Everybody tells you how great marriage can be, but nobody explains the intricacies involved in marriage practically.

Before I got married, things were going well, and I had fewer responsibilities. After I got married, I was confronted with new responsibilities I hadn't met before. Before my marriage, I was working to fulfil my passion. Afterwards, I started working harder because I wanted to give my wife everything she wanted. I had to manage my time and balance between giving attention to my business and my married life, which was difficult at first.

Still, after I explained how I felt about my business, my wife actually understood and helped me balance my life better. In a way, marriage provided me with stability as it brought balance to my life and enabled me to progress at a steady rate - it provided me with the comfort that my partner was waiting to welcome me back home once I got done with a demanding workday.

When I got married, I felt that there was tremendous pressure at first. I was investing in property, progressing in my business, and educating myself. However, my wife really helped and supported me through that time. She is such a brilliant woman, and I have learned so much from her. She has honed so many systems of sign language that enable her to maintain a solid social network, which she helped me tap into as well. I find myself exceptionally lucky because even during the busiest times of my life, my wife has provided me with relief; she has been my go-to person since day one.

I'm very passionate about my business, and so is my wife. However, she is a very astute businesswoman in her field, and our business interests are quite different, so we don't share business-centred interactions. Instead, we cherish the similarities that we have, which enables us to fall in love with our differences.

I've had a very positive experience with my partner when it does come to business. In fact, thanks to her powerful social network in the deaf community, I have been able to secure significant contacts and maintain relationships in the deaf community, which help me in my public speaking by increasing my audience and improving the understanding I share with them. It is vital to support your partner when it comes to their career, and it is okay to ask for help when you are concerned about your own. Marriage is a two-way street; you must give respect, love, and support to receive it.

When I speak about marriage with my audience, I always tell them that before getting married, think about your partner, observe your compatibility, and if you are in a development phase of your career, do try to reach a stable point before getting married. The reason is, as an entrepreneur, you share a very significant relationship with your business. So if you have just gotten married and you're trying to launch a new business at the same time, you are practically juggling two new relationships, both of which require a great deal of time and attention to flourish.

I found it very difficult to manage both my relationship and new businesses efficiently at the same time. This is why my advice is to focus on your personal growth before stepping into such a significant role as someone's spouse because while that brings comfort and joy, it also brings forth many new responsibilities.

However, it is essential to remember that every individual is different, and so is their relationship with both their partner and career. So it is always the person who knows what is best for them; I can only tell you to follow your heart and utilise your mind to make the right decisions at the right time.

I completed my degree from the University College of Central England, now known as Birmingham City University (BCU). My degree was in business and marketing.

When I began my studies at the university, I met the university's official disabled support advisor, who was fantastic and helped me throughout my years at college. They provided deaf students with interpreters, electric note-takers, etc. While BCU was not home to a large population of deaf students, it was pretty sensitive towards our needs and met them to the best of their abilities. Most of the time.

However, that does not imply that gaining my degree was easy. It was anything but that.

For starters, I did not even know that we would have a different lecturer for every other course; I had not prepared for this. While this may seem like an ordinary shift in plans to a hearing individual, it meant more than that because, as a profoundly deaf student, I had to pay extra attention to and remember how each of our tutors spoke and behaved. After all, I did most of my learning through a thorough understanding of body language.

Moreover, in university, I had a timetable that I followed strictly. It allowed me to increase organisation and keep up with my progress. The tutors provided all the students with their respective timetables. I would always make sure that the interpreter arrived, but sometimes I would miss some information, nonetheless. For instance, when I would have to watch the presentation that a teacher had prepared, I would have to keep looking back and forth between the presentation and the interpreter. At times, the interpreter had not even watched the video themselves, which meant they could not translate the entire presentation correctly. Then I would have to ask for details without attaining a helpful answer because I was then asked to concentrate on the presentation even though the presentation would not even have subtitles! This meant that I only had access to body language as a means of communication, unlike other students who could hear and interpret for themselves. So, when I was confronted with jargon in lessons, I would find myself becoming increasingly confused as the interpreter could not guide me, and neither could I self-learn from the video.

Next, I had to face the obstacle of speed. Our lectures were so very fast-paced that the interpreter could not keep up. Then, they would refuse to interpret further, which would cause me several issues because then I would become demotivated as I could not learn as fast as other students could. Even though I campaigned and spoke with the dean, they never resolved this issue. Explaining my situation to the course director did not help either. Still, I did not give up. I talked to the disabled support adviser, and I remember that we had a big meeting about it. He explained that it was just too difficult for them to solve all these issues at the time. I understood where they were coming from, but that did not mean that these problems stopped affecting me. I just accepted that I would have to learn to overcome them on my own.

When I was finally awarded my degree, I felt so proud and relieved that all my hard work had paid off. All the students at our university had gracefully managed to graduate, including pupils attaining their undergraduate, master's, Ph.D. degrees as well. It was a huge graduation ceremony held in a building called National Indoor Arena, which is a big concert hall in Birmingham. We needed the space, as all the students graduating that year were present. I felt proud of myself, and that feeling of achievement helped me realise how important education is. I thought back to when I was sixteen, and I had gotten my first job. I thought about what it would have been like if I had just stayed at that job and continued to work my way ahead instead of gaining a proper education. Evidently, it would have taken me a long time and greater effort to get to where I wanted to be, which was the CEO of my own company. My degree paved the way for me and became a staple of my achievement. I had my path laid out for me, and as I looked ahead at so many students in the graduation hall that night, I wondered what the next step would be for them. I pondered - what would they do with their degrees? Had they thought about who they wanted to be? I was worried about them but excited simultaneously because that day was the start of so many success stories.

As soon as I completed my degree, I began to work on starting my own business right away. I did not know how it would go, but the completion of my degree had given me the confidence to trust myself.

It has been incredibly hard; every day can be difficult. For instance, whenever I go to a big company for an important meeting, every member of that very meeting is hearing. It is not easy to communicate with them. At first, I would try to pitch products to them, but they would reject me, and after failing multiple times, I realised that maybe they could not trust me because I was deaf and that they really did not understand or accept my capabilities. It took time, and now people know who I am; they have begun to trust me. It took a lot of time to get to where I am today because I am deaf, but I did not let my disability define me. And now that I am here, I can see that the wait was worth it.

I overcame each obstacle step by step. In terms of communicating with my clients, I can either speak with them through emails and interpreters on phone calls. If it is ever a deaf client, then I can meet them face to face and communicate with them through sign language. But it is mostly hearing clients, and I am the only deaf person in the room, so in that case, I must rely on book interpreters, especially for board meetings, and events, etc. They become my access to a good conversation that I can then be an active part of.

Today, when I speak to audiences of young people, especially groups of individuals at critical ages of 16-18, I tell them what I will advise all my readers. Do what you feel is right for you, and let your gut guide you. Always plan everything, and set goals, but do not be afraid to take calculated risks to achieve those goals.

However, don't blame me if you choose something that isn't right for you because the only person who knows what's best for you is you.

Many individuals struggle with recurring failure; perhaps it is because they do not even know what success means to them. They do not take the time to determine what they want out of life, and if you do not know where you want to go, you will never take the right route to get there. The crux of the matter is that you should know precisely what you want. Even if you do not have all the details yet, you need a definite goal to work toward.

What does success look to you?

If you do not know the answer to this very question, then you will undoubtedly attract a great deal of confusion into your life.

However, one thing is for sure; success is not what others tell you it is. It is what you believe it is. Suppose you believe success is what everyone else says it is. In that case, you will never gain true satisfaction as authentic contentment comes from attaining what you think is right for yourself. When you achieve someone else's version of success, it will not mean as much to you because you will be living their dream. However great their vision may be, it will never make you happy because it was never yours to keep.

Gaining success takes courage. It necessitates giving up every other belief surrounding the idea of success than the one you hold close to your heart. You need to abandon other people's ideas of success and stop comparing yourself with them. Many individuals are captivated by the belief that prosperity is represented by infinite wealth, glory, and tangible possessions. While financial stability should always be a goal for you, the reality is that success is determined in many ways by many different people. But it must be born within you as a desire and willingness to drive real success on your terms. By recognising and appreciating who you are and why you aspire to win, it automatically becomes more effortless to tap into your existing skills as it makes you more aware of your power, potential, and present knowledge.

What is your definition of success? Do you truly know why you want to succeed? For instance, when you say, "I want success!" what do you really mean by that? What drives you to do better? What is your end goal?

You may assume that success is characterised by capital, prestige, comfort, tangible assets, etc. However, success does not come with a one-size-fits-all label. Success must be determined by your own labels.

The essence of success is diverse for each individual. You may find yourself unable to fit into other people's definition of success, which is why you must understand that every individual has their own purpose to fulfil in life. Once you find yours, you will become more at ease. You must follow your gut. Success is an exclusive concept. The sooner you enable yourself to accept that, the faster you will be able to define and devise your own success story, which will become a blueprint for you to follow throughout your career. After creating a personal blueprint for yourself, you will find it easier to create success on your own terms.

Many people desire to start a business but postpone the decision while searching for the perfect business idea to pop up that will guarantee millions. Most of the time, the sole reason many emerging entrepreneurs don't take action to fulfil their planned goals and dreams is a lack of confidence in their abilities. The only answer to this dilemma is to start right away, just like I did.

Everyone would be a whole lot richer if they knew exactly how to succeed at something or how to accomplish all their goals without the risk of failure. You do not need to figure it all out before you start. I personally believe that just about anyone can gain success at just about anything — when they set their mind to it. If the first step you took was not the right one, learn to bounce back. Readjust. Take another step in a new direction and try again. Don't give up. If I had given up all those years ago, when my life had become challenging as I am profoundly deaf, I would not have been where I am today.

Imagine that you have an inbuilt friend within you who will never allow you to give up. Wouldn't you be able to achieve more? Of course, you would. You are that friend, and it is my advice to you to never ever give up on something you truly believe in.

If every other entrepreneur gives into self-doubt in a dark moment of despair, then we would be left with far less intriguing success stories because failure is the first step towards success. Remember that.

Chapter 6

The Communication Barrier

As individuals ease through daily life activities at home, work, and in social or business situations, necessary auditory abilities prove practical significance. Audition enables an individual to detect and recognise meaningful environmental sounds, identify the source and location of a sound, and, most importantly, observe and comprehend spoken language.

An individual's ability to carry out auditory tasks in the real world is influenced not only by their hearing abilities but also by a mass of situational factors, such as background noise, opposing signals, room acoustics, and awareness of the situation. These elements are vital regardless of whether one has a hearing loss, but the consequences of their absence are magnified when hearing is impaired. For instance, when an individual with a complete hearing ability engages in conversation in a discreet, well-lit setting, visual signals from the speaker's face, along with situational cues and linguistic context, can inject ease into communication. In contrast, in a noisy environment, with low lighting and limited visual cues, it may become challenging to sustain a conversation or give and receive information accurately. An individual with hearing loss may be able to function very well in the former situation but may not communicate at all in the latter.

Individuals who are hard of hearing or profoundly deaf can perform as well as their counterparts with hearing abilities when even-handed educational and employment opportunities are provided. These equitable opportunities depend on the individual student or worker having access to the information necessary for learning or getting the job done. The access to meaningful communication depends on individual needs and the auxiliary aids prepared to approach these needs. For instance, a deaf person who cannot use the telephone can use a TTY or computer system to engage in conversation with hearing individuals through telephone or Internet relay systems. These systems enable operators who type or sign the hearing person's spoken words for the deaf caller via video and voice the words typed by the deaf individual or signed phrases for the hearing caller.

In an educational setting, a profoundly deaf individual such as myself with a complete hearing loss is likely to have trouble comprehending what is being told to them. In such situations, communication access is improved through FM systems and other assistive listening devices. These include computerised note-taking systems like the ones I had in university and other helpful devices. On the other hand, communication is often less than clear within the classroom. As I mentioned before, it would always be difficult for me to keep looking back and forth between the presenter and my interpreter during class at university when I could have efficiently utilised that energy to instil the knowledge that was being relayed to me.

Sadly, not every deaf individual has a fool proof plan prepared for their future as I had. It takes years of planning to understand what is right for you for an individual who has no disabilities, so imagine how difficult it must be for a deaf individual to grasp the best method to attain a fruitful career and happy life. The reserve countless employers feel regarding the hiring of deaf individuals does not help the case. Many work functions have put the unskilled deaf worker at a disadvantage. The assumption that we're making here is that education is a crucial factor that promotes occupational entry and mobility for the deaf worker in a business environment. The ordinarily below-average educational achievement of deaf persons proceeds to contribute to vocational barriers, which is why education has always been mandatory for me because I have always been aware that it is that one symbol of achievement that is recognised across the globe.

The deaf community proudly represents itself as an entity that shares its members' common goals and works toward achieving these goals. These goals include, for instance, telecommunications, entertainment access, captioning, sign language, oral interpreting, and accommodations in the work setting. A majority of the deaf community encompasses individuals who have been deaf from birth or very early on in life. Many of these individuals prefer oral communication but perceive themselves as part of the deaf community. Most deaf individuals rely on signed communication or British Sign Language and identify with Deaf Culture. These individuals value British Sign Language as their language, and they tend to depreciate speech when they interact with each other because their words weigh a ton more. Socialisation with other deaf individuals is heavily stressed upon, mainly through local, state, deaf clubs, religious settings, and Deaf festivals.

In the deaf community, hearing loss is not detrimental to socialisation; instead, it brings people with joint issues together and transforms them into one vibrant entity. As indicated by multiple researchers, hearing loss as measured in decibels is not vital for individuals who identify with Deaf Culture. Instead, what is notable is how members of the deaf community link to each other and communicate with each other. We use vision rather than audition to communicate, frequently through sign language, which is indispensable to our daily living.

Many deaf individuals wear hearing aids to alert them to environmental noises at the very least, but an audition is still not primary in their lives. I remember when I had a cochlear implant, while that had provided me with a refreshing experience, it had given me great pain as well. Some deaf individuals appreciate their previous speech and auditory therapy to maximise spoken English abilities. Others may find such exposure stressful and potentially incompetent in providing them with functionally expressive and receptive spoken English skills.

Generally, those who identify with Deaf Culture perceive sign language as the primary tool that provides significant access to speech, communication, and interactive social experiences. As we have a language acquired through vision and a means to education, they do not see themselves as disabled per se? However, many acknowledge having a disability regarding the lack of hearing that entitles them to coverage under the authorities and its provisions for more equal opportunities.

A hearing disability is not as much an issue for us as the disability engendered by society's reluctance to accommodate our needs by providing interpreter services, captioning, and other means of access to communication. This very reluctance of society is what I envision as profoundly disabling.

Education is a critical factor in understanding the employment status of adults with hearing loss. For individuals who have suffered from an early onset of hearing loss, the challenges for acquiring spoken language, improvement of reading skills, and educational accomplishment can result in low job opportunities. These problems, coupled with the requirement of better career guidance, job placement, and training, can lead to inadequate preparation for entering the workforce on a competitive basis.

A positive career outcome is statistically correlated with a deaf individual's educational level, although this relationship does not always indicate a causal linkage.

When hearing loss transpires during adulthood, after concluding formal education and establishing a work history or career, it professes challenges for job performance and future job mobility. As these adults have already acquired the knowledge and skills needed to perform their jobs, their difficulties are related to communication barriers, such as work conditions and employer attitudes.

The term "disability" has been described in several diverse ways over time, which is made quite evident by the differences found in approaches to disability today. The more initial conceptualisation, based on a medical model, inspected disability as a primary consequence of impairment. Therefore, measurement of impairment could be practised, with proper medical criteria, for disability measurement.

A more positive approach entails an emphasis on what an individual with impairment *can* do and the capabilities the person *does* have. The new emphasis is placed on accommodation and restructuring the environment to maximise each individual's functioning in daily life.

These differing perspectives on disability create challenges and apparent inconsistencies in disability determination. For instance, is it reasonable for deaf adults to claim on one hand that they are disabled and hence entitled to accommodations at work? When they simultaneously argue forcefully that hearing loss is not a disability and that the only thing a deaf person cannot do is to hear? We need more generous benevolence in this criterion. To do that, we must build deaf awareness in hearing individuals so that the government can take reformative steps to assist the deaf community in achieving its goals.

On the other hand, it is not all bad. There have been multiple times when I have found myself feeling fortunate for living in England because there is a magnitude of opportunities present here for deaf individuals. However, a maximum effort is required nonetheless. Whenever I speak to younger audiences, I inform them that there is no area in life where you cannot succeed despite putting in a great degree of effort. What truly matters is understanding the extent of effort you need to inject into achieving your goal and then efficiently succeeding in doing just that.

Whether you attain what you desire to achieve or not, in the end, you will always know that you tried your very best and that self-belief is an accomplishment all on its own.

I was once asked to give a speech addressed to the student body at Birmingham City University, and I had not known prior to the event that I would be doing so. I remember standing up on that stage and feeling like the entire world was waiting for me to relay the words of wisdom. However, the only thing I could think of speaking about was that any individual, despite their disabilities and the obstacles standing in their path, can achieve what they desire to put their mind and effort into it. I had been an alumnus of Birmingham City University, and so had my father. It had been quite close to where I lived and remained to be the home of many beautiful memories.

As I stood up on that stage and looked out at the crowds of students who had gathered to attend my speech, I felt overwhelmed with nervousness, excitement, and pride. I had finally reached a point in my career where different people had begun to value me and see me as an individual separate from my disability. It had taken a great degree of time and effort to get here, but I was here now, and I was going to make the best of it.

That speech provided me with the confidence that I had

always needed to become the person I always wanted to be — a risk-taker, confident with his language, and skilled in his entrepreneurship. I used what other people may call my disability to my advantage and enabled it to become my most significant selling point. I am profoundly deaf, but I can hear the words people utter within their hearts; I know what the market desires, and that is how I cater to their needs with utmost perfection. Being able to speak and being appreciated for it taught me that there are no obstacles that I cannot overcome.

This confidence is what keeps me going, despite the never-ending predicaments that life continues to throw our way.

Take the current global situation, for example. Before the pandemic, I travelled the world, went to multiple meetings a day, socialised, and enjoyed a stable income. However, after the pandemic, I have been forced to remain indoors as we are being told that it is not safe for anyone to step outside. Amidst a world crisis, all I can think about is how grateful we all should be for the little things. Now that I see a mask on every face I cross on the street, in the store, or at the bank, I find it almost impossible to communicate with them.

I am a profoundly deaf individual who relies on visuals to communicate. While technology is my saviour, face-to-face communication has become extremely challenging due to the pandemic. People are being forced to stay indoors, as social gatherings have become unacceptable and speeches impossible. There is no point in meeting anyone as I cannot indulge in a conversation with them if they are wearing a mask. The fact of the matter is that if I need to communicate with someone, they have to take off their mask so I can lip-read what they are trying to convey to me. That defeats the entire purpose of wearing a mask in the first place.

I genuinely believe that the government should consider the difficulties caused for deaf or hard of hearing individuals because of mainstream safety measures. If the concern were granted to people equally, the government would develop more innovative preventive measures such as clear visors. I believe clear visors are twice as efficient as protective gear against the coronavirus when compared to masks. They enable deaf or hard-of-hearing individuals to communicate without the hardship that strains my daily life as a profoundly deaf individual amidst a pandemic.

Evidently, I can text, email, or video call any individual I wish to speak to if they have access to the required technology. Still, daily activities like going to the supermarket, bank, or hospital have become an arduous task indeed. Technology has always helped me communicate with hearing people. Still, when I am face to face with someone, it can be extremely challenging to get my point across.

I cannot meet my clients, indulge in conversation with like-minded entrepreneurs, or speak to audiences, which has become a safe space for me. I feel appreciated. I like being in a position where I can provide advice to hundreds of individuals who can actually benefit from it. However, I cannot do that with ease from home. During these trying times, I have decided to relay my story and advice to all of my readers through this book. I believe that my words can, and will, help thousands of individuals gain hope and work towards their goals with greater motivation than before, whether they belong to the deaf community or the hearing world.

There is a moral to every story, and hope is the message I would like to send out through mine.

My favourite college was Solihull College; everyone was very open-minded. They had excellent deaf awareness, and there was a perfect mix of very welcoming and helpful students. I've always had a mainstream education, but many deaf individuals only attend schools made primarily for deaf students. I decided to receive a mixed education, and I could decide because I had a choice.

I had access to mainstream education; many people do not. Often, the deciding factor between mainstream education and specialized education is access and awareness. I had access to mainstream education, and I was aware of its benefits for me. It took me a long time to feel comfortable in college, so I attended four different colleges. I'm glad that I had the opportunity to attend them until I decided which one was the right fit for me, Solihull College. If

I hadn't received an education, I would have had to learn more skills. Education helped me do what I was interested in successfully. I know what I'm doing because I learned how to do it. Education can be the learning of any subject, and I had decided long ago to learn about everything that interested me.

When I give presentations and speeches, I use PowerPoint to display them and organize my topics. When I reach the venue, the first thing I do is ask the tech team whether they have PowerPoint connected. I do not only enjoy giving speeches; I learned a lot about it as well. I wanted to be as communicative with my audience as possible, so I found ways to connect with them on a level where I got through to my audience, and they understood me. I put a great amount of effort into giving speeches because I want to ensure that my audience understands the idiosyncrasies I put forward and the sign language that I use. I have to get through to them, which does take a lot of work, but it's worth it every time.

I went to my daughter's school to give a speech and presentation after receiving the MBE; her school had invited me to share my wisdom with the students. I was very impressed with the number of creative questions thrown my way, which were unlike the ones I received from an older audience. The younger generation is more open to innovation. They aren't afraid to ask for directions to success, which is why I'm excited about the type of futuristic adults these children will become.

When I started public speaking, I used to feel like I needed to warm up before getting into the main topic and delivering practical workshops. I knew that this was the right career path for me when I understood that I enjoyed every part of it. In fact, I usually keep most of my presentations relatively short, so there is enough time left over for my audience to ask me questions because I love answering them, helping them, and aiding them in seeing the world through a new perspective.

I love public speaking because, as a profoundly deaf individual who delivers speeches through sign language, it allows me to build bridges between the hearing community and the deaf community by showcasing sign language in a field where it is unlikely to be found.

When the pandemic began, I realised I had more time to read books, connect with the deaf community on social media and spend time with my family. However, after I had spent time ticking those things off of my list, the pandemic still wasn't over. It's been a somewhat tricky time because international travel still isn't easily attainable, and I need to travel for my business. There are so many different parts of my life that the pandemic has altered, not in a good way. But, I suppose, the only way out of it is to be optimistic about the future and stop dreading the present.

BORN DEAF TO AN MBE

I don't believe in negativity. I don't think people should worry about the economy dying or undergoing a severe downturn because worry is not the way out of this pandemic. You have to be positive; you have to do your research and development until you figure out how to adapt to the new business world and achieve whatever business ventures you still can. It is essential to understand that this is exclusively a temporary condition and that the pandemic will not last forever. One day, it will all go back to normal.

Chapter 7

Deaf Business Services LTD

"The struggle you're in today is developing the strength you need for tomorrow."

"Don't give up."

-Robert Tew

Success stories often speak about certain aspects to a great degree, one of them being challenges. While challenges can stress entrepreneurs out, they have the potential to motivate ambitious newcomers in the business world because each step, whether it turns out to be a mistake or results in perfection, is still a step forward on the path to success.

It is essential to understand that running a successful business and overcoming challenges go hand in hand. In fact, sustaining the willingness and ambition to greet challenges as motivation is half the battle entrepreneurs must be prepared to fight. The ability to take calculated risks, adapt to a dynamic business environment, and admission of one's mistakes is a big part of the other half.

BORN DEAF TO AN MBE

Ego does not exist in the business world. While respect is a two-way street, you must earn it. The world of entrepreneurship is ever-changing and definitely fast-paced. You must have the courage to acknowledge and accept the mistakes you make during the first few years of entrepreneurship and be willing to find efficient solutions in a timely manner in order to succeed.

There is no success story without failure. It can be discouraging to imagine that every step you take during the start-up of your enterprise might be a mistake, but it is also vital to understand that every mistake is a gateway to improvement, and there is no bridge to perfection that you can walk upon without risking drowning in the sea of sorrow below. Risk is a part of every regime; you just have to know how to calculate it and then take the best decision for you and your business.

Every one of us has waded into murky waters now and again, seldom deep enough to make us feel like we may be losing the plot. However, entrepreneurs who cherish what they do never entirely lose sight of the challenge and the sense of purpose that compels them to achieve their goals. They climb their way to the top, no matter how dismal everything gets, because it's the very thing that gets them up in the morning, every single day.

During a crisis, I wish that more people would try to delve into their histories in order to connect with extremely powerful reminders.

If they dig hard enough, they'll find traces to faint memories of what once fuelled their passions, and that motivation is what will enable them to overcome any obstacle that is thrown their way. Do you remember what had you riled up about beginning your own business in the first place? Hold on to that thought, and use it to find your ambition and fuel your success.

The biggest challenge for entrepreneurs is often taking the first big leap. That is the first challenge that they encounter, the battle that they must fight with themselves and attain victory. That first challenge may revolve around quitting your previous job, building a social network, constructing a website, proposing your first pitch, or just announcing your big idea to the world and investing the credit you have.

This typically originates after a reasonable measure of brainstorming and devising. At this time, your mind may play tricks on you. Suspicion and uncertainty may creep into your unconscious mind. You might begin to make plenty of excuses.

The truth is that the timing is always better than you imagine it to be; there is no better time than now.

Big 'overnight' success is actually the culmination of steadfast, consistent little efforts over time. That applies to branding, marketing, and fundraising. Sadly, the immense majority of entrepreneurs double over and quit right before the big pay can take place. If only they had held on for another day, week, or month, everything would have come together. Maybe far better than they ever imagined.

The uncertainty that accompanies entrepreneurship is often demotivating, which is why bracing yourself for the worst, and doing your best is extremely important. Be brave, and don't let aspects such as scary competitors with fat pockets, low funding, or lack of capital make you back off. Even if you're tapping into a market that is already competitive, you have to remind yourself that the pie is big enough for everyone. Be content with your slice but hungry to earn another.

I encountered almost all of the problems, if not more than every entrepreneur is bound to interact with at the beginning of their personal initiative. I learned a lot through practically working in the field because everything looks great on paper but often turns out completely different in real life. However, I do wish that someone – possibly a mentor – would have taught me more about business functions such as marketing, branding, sales, etc.

Hence, when I speak to my audiences, I try to be as authentic as possible. I am successful now and content with where I am, but I am and always will stay hungry for greater success. That's just how entrepreneurs are and should be. However, there was a time when I was in a place most beginning entrepreneurs get stuck at, if not behind them, due to the communication barrier I had to overcome as a profoundly deaf person.

SHEZAD NAWAB

While I had greater experience than the average beginner due to previously shared business projects with my family, I like to say that I was relatively clueless. I began to understand the business world from an entirely diverse and honest viewpoint the day I stepped into the market and practically began working on my initiative, and I made my fair share of mistakes.

My first business was called Deaf Business Services Ltd.; it was the first company that I set up. The reason why I set this business up was that I had already been working in the international market, property development with my family, but I wanted this to be my own initiative. It would be personal, which would motivate me to a greater degree and empower me on another level.

The ideology behind Deaf Business Service Ltd. came from my experience of being a profoundly deaf individual and an entrepreneur as well. I wanted to serve the deaf community, and I wanted to do it by providing them with opportunities in the field that I personally admired. I knew that they needed support with entrepreneurship, which is why I set up DBS Ltd.

My vision was to work with the deaf community because we could communicate face-to-face using sign language, which meant greater ease for my deaf clients and me. I had a range of different services that I wanted to offer the deaf community in terms of business strategies, obviously for a profit. Turns out, it wasn't that obvious after all.

At first, I had felt like Deaf Business Services Ltd. was a fairly decent name considering the aim of the company. I began to prepare the branding material for my company, and when everything was ready such as letterheads, business cards, the whole mix, I decided to launch my company and begin pitching its services. I met several people (including individuals from the hearing community) who found it difficult to understand the purpose of my company given its name. At the time, I assumed their misunderstanding was the result of my inability to relay the perfect pitch to them. I also thought, perhaps, they were confused as it's uncommon for a profoundly deaf individual to run their own business on such an optimum level.

However, the problem was - I had not taken into account that the deaf community is a very small market, and the hearing world has a bigger market that I could tap into. While I wanted to work with both of these communities, my name gave off the impression that I only wished to serve the deaf community. I then began to wish that I had thought harder and more practically regarding the name of my company, so I wouldn't look as if I was only selling my services to deaf individuals.

It had been a branding mistake. It took me a long time to understand that branding makes a huge difference in business; it truly hit me where it hurts. I thought that my clientele would understand what I was trying to say, but there was a miscommunication occurring due to my error. People assumed I was only willing to sell my services to deaf people. Thus, by naming my company deaf business services, I had restricted my market approach by limiting people's perceptions regarding my company's purpose and intentions.

Therefore, I had to do a lot of thinking, indulge in a lot of soul searching in order to understand what I wanted to do with my company with certainty. I thought long and hard about what markets I wanted to target, and I really questioned myself about how I wanted to brand this initiative. In the end, I decided that I wanted to sell to both the hearing and deaf community worldwide and that this name would limit my chances of achieving that opportunity.

After I launched the company, provided clients with my business cards, gave presentations, I thought that they would understand that I was willing to provide to both markets, but since the branding hadn't been done efficiently enough at first, people were confused about my business. Therefore, I had to correct the marketing error I was making and rebrand my company by renaming it with a typical business title so both deaf and hearing communities would feel welcomed to purchase my services. That is when I began to receive recognition from both markets.

The reason why I had chosen deaf business limited as a name was because it really spoke to me. I thought it would be unique, it also promoted diversity, so I imagined that it would naturally be a hit amongst both communities. However, it had not done what I had intended to do with it. To fix the damage, I surveyed the market and took a better, practical decision by rebranding my initiative because adapting to consumer preferences in the markets that you want to tap is essential, especially for a start-up to survive and prosper.

When I practically started my business, I was surprised to find that the business world is nothing like the world of college that I had lived in for the past many years, and it was also completely different from the business world I had explored with my family because they were extremely used to interacting with deaf and hearing people which provided them with greater ease. However, doing everything on my own was a new challenge for me - a massive one, indeed. After adding the hearing community to the markets that I wanted to operate in, I understood that there would be massive communication barriers between me and my clients due to my profound deafness and the lack of their ability to use sign language.

I strived for government funding and successfully attained what I needed. That government grant enabled me to hire a freelancer BSL interpreter who could accompany me to business meetings, attend phone calls, interpret letters and presentations, etc. Thanks to the funding that I had attained, I could move into the hearing community and promote my business successfully with ease by booking an interpreter for every business activity needed.

Deaf Business Services Ltd. was supposed to be a private limited company. However, when I would network with hearing people during the time my company still had that name, they would become confused and begin to think that due to the disability mentioned in the title of my company that it was a charity or a social enterprise. Then I would have to explain profusely that that was not the case at all as my company was a private limited entity. Therefore, this particular crisis helped me understand that if you add the name of any kind of disability, it makes your organisation sound a lot more like a charity. It's honestly a perception most normally abled individuals possess when the reality is quite the opposite. Your disability does not define you, which is why naming something after it can also speak about your success with dealing with a specific disability rather than your struggle.

When I figured out most people don't think that way, it became a learning curve for me, and the reason why I say my branding failed at first. Then, I thought long and hard about how I should rebrand my business and what I wanted to make different this time. After a careful review from my newly born perspective of the business world, I changed my brand name to management consulting, which helped me relay an instant message to potential clients regarding what I do.

I think it's crucial for entrepreneurs to understand that every project and plan comes with a certain level of risk. It took me time and experience to realise that everyone can make mistakes, and it is normal for entrepreneurs to mistake a project as risk-free. When I began my first company and came face-to-face with a branding issue, I began to understand how much research goes into creating a lucrative business that clearly communicates its message to clients. It helped me understand that every project has an accompanying risk, but one can minimise that risk by focusing their energy on research and development.

The biggest mistake that I've made in the past is branding. When working in the west, a big part of branding is your hold on the English language. English is my second language, and I'm a profoundly deaf individual, making it difficult for me to communicate the meaning behind my business. When I explained the purpose of my business and highlighted its unique selling point, I observed that the deaf audience understood me well, given that I was communicating with them using sign language. But, the hearing audience remained confused. Later, I figured that even with an interpreter, it could be difficult to get your message across to a hearing audience because they are not aware of the jargon or technical language used in sign language. This communication barrier can be challenging to comprehend even after being translated. I learned that creating a solid communication link with your clients is essential because they keep your business afloat. The key to good communication is to work twice as hard to ensure it is clear, persuasive, and understood.

When clients spoke directly to me, they understood what my services offered; they could comprehend that I offered business consultancy, development, and support. The basic services I provided were high-powered, highly demanded, and well thought out, but we found it difficult to communicate these strengths to our clients due to the branding issue. However, after reviving our branding and beginning a new campaign, I observed the difference it brought to our sales. It taught me the importance of communication, branding, and staying connected with clients.

Setting up my first business was anything but easy; I was a one-person band, and I was working alone. However, I was spreading my business through word of mouth in both deaf and hearing communities. Goodwill always profits you in the long run. Write that down. I knew social media was an excellent tool for marketing, but I didn't have much awareness about it in the beginning, but then I gained that awareness and established a hold over it. It helped my business significantly, and I noticed how marketing, including social media marketing, can benefit businesses massively. It is essential to follow the technological advancements in the business world and learn to stay linked with clients in every market, whether it is virtual or physical.

When I was younger, I knew with conviction that I could

achieve great things in life. While that confidence did help me prosper, it also became tainted when I realised how difficult it is for a profoundly deaf individual to attain success in a hearing world. However, I gained my confidence by working twice as hard and achieving my dreams despite my challenges. Easy success isn't real success; real success is always earned.

I think one of the challenges that sole entrepreneurs face is the difficulty that accompanies working alone. For example, when I have to take calls with hearing clients or hold meetings with them, I need to book an interpreter beforehand, or I cannot take those calls or attend these meetings, which is why it takes twice as much planning and hard work to work alone, but then success feels twice as better. I know my challenges, but I have learned how to overcome them because I have spent a great deal of time and energy learning about these challenges and how I can conquer them. Entrepreneurs need three skills:

- Problem Solving Skills.

- Adaption. For example, book an interpreter before a meeting if you're a deaf individual or find another communication method because business must go on as usual.

- Team Building. Even if you work alone, you will need another partner, subordinate, or team member to work with you, such as the second pair of eyes to look over written drafts in a foreign language to ensure that you communicate clearly with your clients. Remember, better safe than sorry. If you don't have another team member to help you, then take the help of other trusty resources.

My advice to all my readers is to reach within themselves and find the venture that matches their purpose. First, you must connect to your business. Figure out what type of company you wish to create, plan its development through every stage, tackle the obstacles on your way, and stick to your goals. It would be best if you believed in yourself and in your business to become a successful entrepreneur. After all, how will you persuade another client to buy your product or service if you don't see the purpose of buying them yourself?

Think about it.

Here are my two pence;

Before you set up your business, make sure you do your market research. Conduct market surveys, ask people you trust about the name of your company. You can never have too much advice, only if you know which one to follow. Make sure your branding communicates the message you want it to. Find a business mentor so you don't have to go back and forth due to petty mistakes or waste your time and energy trying to fix them. Indulge in thinking, creativity, passion, research service or product, make a checklist, get a calendar, mark it, and start working.

As I said, I made my fair share of mistakes, but I knew all

along that no matter how drastic things get, giving up wasn't an option. It shouldn't be for you either because mistakes do waste your time and energy, but there is no success without failure. Falling teaches you how to get back up, which is why there is no better gateway to improvement than making mistakes and learning how to kill them the next time.

Chapter 8
No Experience in Diversity Business

"An individual has not started living until he can rise above the narrow confines of his individualistic concerns to the broader concerns of all humanity."

-Martin Luther King, Jr

The world would be a better place if everyone learned to live with each other in harmony. However, the world would become a safe space filled with acceptance and creativity if we learned to work and support each other despite our differences.

Diversity is a concept that I was taught to embrace as a child, which became the foundation that supported my vision as an adult. Diversity strives to include individuals with various physiological, racial, ethnic, socioeconomic, geographic, and academic/professional backgrounds. It promotes people with diverse opinions, backgrounds, executive experiences, religious beliefs, corporate backgrounds, political principles, sexual orientations, heritage, and life experiences. As a profoundly deaf individual, diversity became my principle, and I have studied it to the core in order to find the best method to incorporate it into a collaboration opportunity that I could share with a range of business organisations.

So, what is diversity?

The definition of diversity refers to the presence of different characteristics in a group of people. These characteristics could be everything that provides them with their own identity and make them unique, such as their cognitive skills, personality traits, and various elements that form their personality (e.g., race, age, gender, religion, sexual orientation, cultural background).

To adequately understand and define diversity, we can reflect on it in a social context. For illustration, at work, you might interact with co-workers of different genders, age groups, faiths, and so on. That is diversity.

Diversity is any dimension that an organisation can use to distinguish groups and personalities from one another. In a nutshell, it concerns individuals' empowerment by not only recognising but also welcoming and appreciating what makes them different in terms of age, gender, ethnicity, creed, disability, sexual orientation, education, background, and national origin.

Diversity supports the exploration of these differences in a secure, confident, and nurturing environment. It involves understanding one another by transcending simple tolerance to warrant people to value their differences genuinely. It enables us to embrace and celebrate the rich dimensions of diversity within each individual and place value on diversity in the community and the workforce.

Each individual in an organisation carries a diverse set of perspectives, work, life experiences, and religious and cultural differences. One can only unleash the power of diversity and reap its benefits when one recognises these differences and learns to respect and value each individual's irrelevant background. Through my organisation's work ethic, I wanted to help instil inclusion, respect, and recognition across the entire workforce.

However, when I began working with a diverse strategy, I discovered that diversity does not arise in our conscious minds but from our hearts. It isn't some technique; it is an art. My vision behind building a diverse organisation was embedded in my desire to promote acceptance, management, and leadership creativity and innovation entrepreneurship in the global diversity workplace. While diversity had always been an essential tool for me since the beginning of my entrepreneurship, I found that very few individuals were aware of its advantages, which forged a direct link to economic prosperity.

It is popularly perceived that diverse teams lead to more

innovative and practical approaches and implementation. The reasoning behind this is essentially straightforward. Innovative thinking naturally compels individuals to work outside of the typical paradigms of operation, employing diverse perspectives to craft original and novel conclusions. A group of comparable individuals with focus skills is less likely to stumble across a range of new ideas that may direct to innovative progress than a group of individuals who enjoy different perspectives, opinions, and ideas. Indeed, similarity cultivates groupthink, which abbreviates creativity.

In a competitive marketplace, a company that employs a diverse workforce can adequately understand the demographics of the global consumer marketplace it serves and is, therefore, sufficiently equipped to thrive in that marketplace than a corporation with a confined range of employee demographics. Amidst the emerging markets across the globe illustrating actual gross domestic product (GDP) and market growth, organisations demand local talent to enter the marketplace and communicate persuasively. Individuals from a particular region will have a profound awareness of the market gaps, consumer preferences and demands in that region, and similar culture which will enable them to add considerable value to their organisation's strategy development.

Organisations must be flexible in the modern economy, as this can be critical in promptly reacting to competitive dynamics and staying ahead of the industry trends. Diversity facilitates out-of-the-box thinking and refined decision-making through a more profound and comprehensive worldview. Diversity also approves the hiring of various individuals with diverse skill sets, creating a larger talent pool for organisations to choose from and employ. The usefulness of this, especially at the managerial level, is tremendous. It has forever been essential for organisations to be adaptable. There has never been a better time to leverage the strength of diversity and use it to promote harmonious unity and unshakeable strength.

During my study on diversity, I learned that there are four kinds of it, and they can all be utilised to promote acceptance in the global workplace. The first type of diversity, which is also the most difficult for most people to wrap their heads around, is internal diversity, which includes diverse characteristics such as race or physical ability. I have always been internally diverse, and as a profoundly deaf individual with great willingness and a dream to prove how diversity can pave a pathway to achievements, I find that to be my greatest strength.

Then, there is external diversity which includes aspects such as an individual's citizenship or education. The last two types of diversity are organisational and worldview diversity. Organisational diversity, also known as functional diversity, is related to the dissimilarities between people that are allocated to them by an organisation — fundamentally, these are the characteristics within a workplace that separate one employee from another. On the other hand, worldview diversity speaks about the different perspectives that individuals possess about the world that they live in and the environment that they function within.

As far as I've learned, worldview diversity is an amalgamation of all three types of diversities and a natural result of being a diverse individual. If you recognise your identity as one that is unique or different, you must also perceive the world in a different light. From my perspective, diversity is the ability to share our differences, and that has always been my secret to success.

On the other hand, I would like to acknowledge that it is anything but easy to promote a corporately diverse organisation because it is difficult for most people to understand or relate to. This makes it even more challenging to find investors who are willing to get on board with your ideas and inject their capital into your mission. I often experienced a disconnection with a majority of the people I pitched my ideas to, and the reason behind that was their lack of awareness towards diverse individuals and the benefits of diversity for everyone. A lack of awareness breeds a lack of acceptance. Therefore, it is natural for people to oppose your idea simply because it is different from what they have encountered in their experiences so far.

It is imperative for you to stay strong during such uncertain times and never give up. If you continue to believe in your ideas and support your vision with a willingness to fulfil your mission, then you will rise above the chaos just like I did. It may take more time and greater effort, but if you don't give up, you will get to your destination sooner or later.

I have always loved being different, and the desire to construct a diverse organisation often drove me to study various organisational structures and understand their concept. During this time, I came across a few highly interesting concepts such as SME's, blue-chip companies, and family offices.

In the world of investment, a blue-chip company is reputable, authenticated, and well-capitalised. Such a company is considered a leading company in its sector and offers a range of dominant goods or services. Blue-chip companies are usually adequately prepared to survive during economic downturns due to their consistent revenues and steady growth over time. They are often household names known to the general public rather than just investors or enthusiasts.

I wanted my company to qualify as a blue-chip organisation that possessed the ability to break through communication barriers like a small- to mid-size enterprise (SME), a corporation with resources, assets, or numbers of employees below a certain level to enhance business communication within the organisation. After figuring out what I wanted, I studied family offices which are private wealth management advisory firms that assist ultra-high-net-worth individuals (UHNWIs). They are different from commonwealth management operations as they offer an outsourced solution to managing an affluent individual or organisation's finances. That is the kind of financial assistance I decided I needed if I wanted financial security to be a characteristic investor remembered my company by.

See, when I speak about diversity, I do not only mean individualistic diversity but also diversity as a whole—the art of being unique, not only as an individual but also as an organisation. You can alter your business structure, characteristics, and strengths to create an environment that is different from other corporations. This can benefit you as it provides you with your own distinct identity, and we all know how important that is for every organisation.

At the end of the day, the obstacles that I struggled with and overcame were a result of my lack of experience concerning diversity in an organisational setting, which is why I always encourage my audience and readers to do their research and learn to adapt to the dynamic business environment we all function within.

Diversity in the workforce creates various opportunities. People from different ethnic backgrounds bring their personal business ethics with themselves, providing the organisation with a chance to change their outlook and working style. These individuals possess distinct creative ideas, and that workplace becomes a focal point for rich streams of innovative knowledge and specialised skills to flow towards.

This allows an organisation to absorb innovative ideas and adopt a different perception. In fact, diversity also enables organisations to build a good rapport with their clients who really care about what kinds of employees the company hires, whether they are biased in any way and if these employees are well taken care of.

I believe with conviction that the future will reveal an advanced rate of diversity in the global workforce, and I want to see diverse groups coming to light for their skills. I fully support every area of diversity; I would like to see new brilliant faces climbing corporate ladders, shattering the glass ceiling, and coming out as CEOs, directors, and overall high achievers. In addition, I want to see a more significant number of deaf individuals, women, people of colour, and members of the LGBTQ+ community excel in the global workforce and be given credit for their effort and creativity.

Perhaps, people find it difficult to find their footing when it comes to diversity. Maybe, they find it challenging to bring in a more diverse workforce. The best way to bring in a competent, diverse workforce is through business networking. There are so many diverse, skilled and innovative individuals in your business-socio circle who could help you change the course of history by evolving along with your business. Go for it.

My experience tells me that the best way to learn about a field is to jump right into it with both your feet. This will enable you to learn about the field you wish to work in on-field first-hand. There is no better teacher than experience. So don't worry about gaining too much experience before you begin working in a field, do complete your market research, and be prepared but don't think that you cannot excel in a field simply because you lack the experience for it. You can create new experiences and learn from them. I've expanded my knowledge and skill by sharing meaningful conversations with experts, training on-site, and being passionate about what I do. So, in my experience, it is much better to learn on the job and make your way from there.

My favourite memory from Buckingham Palace is actually going right into the palace and being able to experience history first hand. There are so many awe-inspiring historic antiques placed within the palace, but my favourite was the classic collection of art that adorned the walls and created a picturesque scene. Observing the art collected by royals throughout various historical stages enables one to see into their mind and understand their perception. I thoroughly enjoyed looking through that window into the history of the United Kingdom.

This memory reminds me of how I achieved success despite

my troubles and helps me inspire others facing similar challenges to work harder and smarter. If there is a will, there is a way; always remember that.

Chapter 9

The Day of the MBE

"It's not about whether you win or lose; it's about how you play the game."

"No matter who you are, what the colour of your skin is, and what obstacles stand in your path, never give up on your journey to success."

You must never give up. It is your duty to keep going, keep striving. Do you remember when you were just a child? You had so many hopes and dreams; it is your responsibility to fulfil the hopes and dreams that you had as a child. You owe it to yourself.

There will be many times in life when you will find yourself unable to go on. You will feel weak, shattered, and exhausted. You will have to realise how easy it is to give up and how difficult it will be to keep going. Nevertheless, you will keep going because you are strong. It would be best if you believe in yourself. There will come a day when you will be glad you chose to keep fighting because that was when you truly began winning.

The MBE refers to a Member of the British Empire. On 16th March 2017, I received it for my services to the sector of business and diversity.

In November 2016, I was working as usual. I reached home a bit late and found a big, heavy envelop on my desk. At first, I was confused. Was this a fine? Was it from the taxing office? Was it a legal document? Well, it had my name on it, so I had to open it. In the beginning, all I could see was an expanse of small text which, when I looked closer, became the most excellent news I had ever received.

My mother and sister heard me scream for joy, and my entire family gathered around me to read the letter that stated I would be receiving an MBE. My parents, siblings, and my wife all read the letter carefully and expressed their joy. However, we were strictly told that this letter was completely confidential for the next six weeks. It would be announced on New Year's eve's honour list.

On New Year's Eve, I was getting ready to take a holiday with my family, but my father called and told me how the honours list was all over the newspapers, and my name was in the list in all of the greatest newspapers that we had grown up reading. It was only a matter of time before I started receiving countless letters congratulating me. Yet, all I could think about was who had nominated me?

BORN DEAF TO AN MBE

Two days before 16th March 2017, when I received the MBE, the Mayor invited my wife and me to afternoon tea. It was a small, festive gathering with everyone from Solihull who had received an MBE or an OBE, so I had a great time networking with these diverse yet like-minded individuals.

The Mayor and his wife were a fantastic couple who interacted with and spoke to everyone at the gathering that evening. Although I had imagined that the mayor would be a strict, straightforward gentleman, I was surprised because he was nothing like that. He was truly hilarious. He had a great sense of humour, and he was very kind.

So, after they announced that I would be receiving an MBE, I asked the Mayor's wife who had nominated me? And, she said that her lips were sealed for eternity. It was quite a jolly evening, one that I'll remember forever. Ever since I have received this award, I have spent quite a bit of time trying to solve the mystery of my secret nominator.

On 16th March 2017, I began my preparations to start the day by getting dressed. I had special instructions regarding what to wear and when to arrive. I wore a dark, brilliant shade of purple with a handkerchief in my top pocket. The palace was actually quite far since I lived in Birmingham and we had to drive to London, which took about two hours. We had been told strictly to reach before ten, so we were aiming to reach by half-past nine.

Once we arrived, thankfully on time, they conducted an entire inspection, with a proper police convoy in place. They then gave each of us something like a visitor's card that proved the police had already searched us. Our passports were then checked. We travelled underground through two sets of doors; we then drove into a big white square to park our car.

Everyone had their own specific car park. We weren't allowed to carry our phones; we were perfectly happy to respect the rules. When we arrived inside, it was absolutely breathtakingly beautiful. There were gigantic sculptures that lined the palace walls, real size portraits, and I can't help but say incredible architecture. I had a little practice; we had a walk-through. Then, I met Prince Charles. I still remember; I felt actual goosebumps. We had a great chat, and I was surprised to find that it didn't feel as formal as I had expected it to be. He's a great person. I had never thought I'd be in Buckingham Palace, let alone meet Prince Charles, so it all felt quite surreal. I had the opportunity to mark it off my bucket list without even knowing that it had been there all this time.

When I was a young boy, I'd go sightseeing with my parents; we'd spend our afternoon looking at the museums, historical architecture and enjoying the picturesque sight of London. I remember feeling wowed at the sight of Buckingham Palace. I can recall looking at Buckingham Palace and knowing that that is where the Queen lives. I always thought about how it would feel going inside the palace.

And, I finally found out. Stepping into the palace felt like a dream, a dream that came true. When I had first seen that letter, I had felt so overwhelmed, I had thought, oh my goodness, I am actually going to go into the palace I had always thought about as a child, and once I had made it inside it, it began to feel like all of my hard work was finally paying off. I was glad that I hadn't given up.

My award became a massive thing in my family. I had the entire spotlight to myself. I loved sharing it with my grandmother, uncles, aunts, cousins, nieces, and nephews. I loved the confidence it gave them; the power my journey gave them. It really shocked many people, but I was happy to be an inspiration for the deaf community because my success proved that anyone could achieve whatever they wanted to despite any disabilities, obstacles, or problems that stood in their path.

When I arrived at Buckingham Palace to receive my MBE, I was amongst a wide range of people. A majority of these individuals receiving various awards were white, but many of them were people of colour from different ethnicities. I was surprised to find that I was among the youngest entrepreneurs present to receive an award; most participants were between the ages of thirty-five to seventy. As a

Muslim Asian profoundly deaf entrepreneur, I did not feel singled out. In fact, I saw a very diverse crowd come together to celebrate their successes despite their ethnicities, backgrounds, age, or gender. It was a proud moment to see so many people be handed a reminder for their achievements in the form of an award, and I was glad to share mine with like-minded individuals.

I loved observing the statues, the art, and the portraits adorned on the walls of Buckingham Palace. It felt surreal and almost dream-like. It was a day I will never forget, as that was when I learned that true success does exist, and nothing feels better than knowing that you've achieved it and yet, have so much more to learn. Being appreciated for your hard work helps you feel motivated, so remember to tell yourself that you're doing okay.

After I received my MBE, I noticed that it impacted my business a great deal. I was invited to several interviews, requested more meetings, and witnessed significant growth in my clientele. I also noticed a growth in my international clientele as well. So, to all the entrepreneurs out there, I want you to know that you can be heard through word of mouth, you will be appreciated, and you can get out there with your products or services and succeed. It's not easy, but it is possible, all you have to do is believe in yourself and your business, and you'll already be halfway there.

I had never even imagined the success I had received. When I started, all I had was a bit of experience and a whole lot of passion. It pushed me to do better and never stop learning how to do it. I have realised that you can never have enough experience or wisdom when it comes to the market because the business world is dynamic and ever-changing. Therefore, you must keep learning to become adaptable and successful.

If I had not adapted to the advancement of technology or the changing world around me, I would not have been able to connect with emerging brilliant minds worldwide or share my services in international markets as we do now through social media networking. There are so many untraditional, innovative ways to begin, maintain and run your business these days. And, the best part is that they work if you execute them right. Success is a small step away if you refuse to stop learning and continue working smart. You will be appreciated and rewarded for your smart work, but you must appreciate yourself before anyone else.

My story acts as evidence that you can and you will achieve your dreams; you simply have to believe in them.

Chapter 10

The Hustle Never Ends

My name is Shezad Nawab (MBE), and I am profoundly deaf.

My father was from Malawi, my mother was from Pakistan, and my grandfather was from India. I was born and raised in Birmingham, United Kingdom. I have journeyed through countless roadblocks, tackled various challenges, and overcome a great number of predicaments. Today, I am recognised as an entrepreneur who grew beyond the conventional boundaries of individuals who struggle with a disability.

I have received many prestigious awards, including Ummul Mu'minin Khadijah Award for Excellence in Enterprise, 2018, Alumni of the Year 2017 in the field of Enterprise and Innovation, Member of the Order of the British Empire (MBE) in the New Year 2017, and made it to the Honours list for services to business and diversity. In addition, I was shortlisted for Young Achiever of the Year, 2016; listed in the top 10 Most Influential Disabled People in Business, 2014, received the Business Initiative Award, 2011, presented with the Young Entrepreneur Award, 2011, and Innovation Voucher Winner, 2010.

BORN DEAF TO AN MBE

I am a specialist in management consulting; I enjoy supporting business ideas and enabling them to grow. I work as an interim executive director, C-level, Chairman, Non-Executive / Board Level Director, where I look over risk assessment, performance, strategic organisation, and people. I am also an international speaker, and I am invited to various business presentations, seminars, and workshops where I teach learners how to build their business empires. I have been actively involved in supporting several new businesses and start-ups over the last seventeen years as well as working with SMEs to help them grow their businesses. During my travel to various parts of the world, I mastered six different sign languages – British, American, Arab, South African, Moroccan, and International.

If you'd like to know what I really do, I'd say that I help entrepreneurs take their business to the next level. I teach them how to form business plans, practising on the pitch whilst maintaining clarity, efficiency, business organisation structure, and precision. I delve into the depth of every business and enable its owners to recognise its specialty again. Establishing a business and then enabling it to grow isn't an easy task. There are several things to keep in mind when preparing a business plan or to prepare a pitch, such as an overview/snapshot of the business, leadership and management, team description/roles, and financials. I help individuals find investors; I involve myself in the preparation of their pitch when they're ready to begin selling their product or service. I talk to them about the kind of people they want as partners; I tell them to trust their gut. After all, business is entirely based on trust. It is my job to ask questions like, what kind of a partner do you want? What kind of team do you need? What stage is your business currently at, and what stage do you want it to reach? I travel to several parts of the world, delivering interactive workshop training that is accessible for deaf and hearing people.

I have experience of seventeen years of running small businesses. There is so much that goes into the start-up of a small business; there's an entire step-by-step process to follow. So many individuals aren't aware of the right process to follow, what steps to take, how to brand the product, copyrighting, etc. I look at start-ups as learners, and I love teaching them how to go about building a successful start-up. I pay extra attention to entrepreneurs who follow their passion, who are ambitious about their work, just like I am. I want to help these people; I want to support deaf business owners, entrepreneurs who struggle with a disability, freelancers, etc. I wanted to support the community I was born into.

I am an activist for deaf people's rights, and when I started my businesses, I travelled to many countries, met so many deaf entrepreneurs. I attended their workshops, and I saw the power in their struggle, the glory in their success. I wanted to deliver that knowledge to the rest of the deaf business community, who did not have the opportunity to learn directly from several entrepreneurs as I did. It inspired me to help more people like these and be a part of such an amazing learning experience. With the help of a British Sign Language interpreter person (voice), I spoke about business to a hearing audience at Royal Bank of Scotland / National Westminster Bank, Naidex, SME Live, and many more. The topics I spoke about surrounded business diversity and communication barriers.

I have achieved approximately six or seven different awards for business achievements. I work hard, but I do not do it for the awards. However, when I do receive these awards, it feels like my hard work truly paid off. The MBE I received inspired me to work harder and achieve greater things. I have achieved so many of my goals, but this is just the beginning. That is the attitude I want my readers to share with me. I want you to remember, it is never too late to begin working on your dream, and it is never right to give up on your goals.

You will face a great number of challenges, but you will overcome them with time, patience, and hard work. There is one tip that helped me achieve my goals, and I call it the three T's of success; Time, Today and Tomorrow. Time refers to time management. Involve time management in every move you make, schedule every single meeting, and plan everything to the minute. Today denotes what you have planned for that very moment and what you want to achieve in the present? Don't stop until you have made progress in your mission to achieve whatever it is that gets your blood thumping. And, finally, tomorrow. What's your next step? Always plan for tomorrow when you're planning for today, and ensure that what you're planning for tomorrow can be done today.

The right entrepreneur understands that true success is unachievable, and that is the beauty of it. It is not about winning or losing, but the time and effort you put into your business. You decide what success means to you, and that is the path that you will choose to follow. We are all working towards a destination, but only a very few individuals realise that it is the journey that truly matters.

Let's get to work.

If you want to set up a business, you have to give it a lot of thought. Are you selling a new invention, or are you delivering a new service? How much time are you willing to put into the business? A year or two?

The thing is, you cannot give up on your project without a definite cause. You should plan long-term and be willing to stick with the program for as long as it takes. You will need to invest time, capital, and energy to help your business grow and evolve. It may take weeks, months, or years, but if you have the right strategy, it will be worth it in the end.

If you're struggling with a skill gap as an entrepreneur, then either learn new skills or bring in a partner who has the abilities you lack and ensure that you possess the abilities they lack. No one is perfect, but two imperfect yet brilliant minds can change the world together. Think about the hours you can give to your business, the effort you are willing to put in, and the changes you are willing to make in yourself and your business. Then, find a partner who can complete your equation because it's okay if you cannot do everything alone. It is alright to ask for help when you need it, but remember to be competent when it's time to return the favour.

The key to achieving fearlessness is never giving up; you must believe in yourself, your ideas, and your business. You have to keep going. You will find it easier to make time, effort, and space to create and innovate your business if you feel passionate about it. So, don't let the spark die out; keep it lit with the fire of your passion.

My motto is, when you earn your own money, don't spend it unwisely. Spend on necessities and maintain a healthy lifestyle, but don't worry about luxurious branded clothes, a flashy car, or a massive mansion. Instead, save money and think about investing; it is essential to slowly but steadily build a financial cushion that you can lean on in financially challenging circumstances.

Before 2019, business was going well. However, in 2020, the business world halted. It made me feel uncertain about the future, but what kept me going was figuring out a way to step around the obstacles in my path and reach my destination relatively unscathed. In times of hardship, it helps if you think positively about the problem at hand and the future that awaits you. Try not to feel disappointed; focus your energy on finding a solution instead.

I'm still on my business journey; I'm still young and keen to keep working and learning about the business world. I don't think age can affect your business life until you let it. If you're still passionate, hardworking, and honest, you will find a way to attain success despite any obstacle in your path. However, it is essential to understand that success isn't a destination. It is the journey you take to reach self-actualisation.

Made in United States
North Haven, CT
13 February 2022